# THE U...
# SPOTTER'S
# HANDBOOK

# Contents

**Part 1** (Wild Flowers) was written by Christopher Humphries and illustrated by Hilary Burn.
**Part 2** (Trees) was written by Esmond Harris and illustrated by Annabel Milne and Peter Stebbing.
**Part 3** (Birds) was written by Peter Holden and illustrated by Trevor Boyer.
Additional illustrations are by Joyce Bee and Christine Howes.
Designed by Sally Burrough. Cover design by Cloud Nine Design.
Edited by Sue Jacquemier.

First published in 1978 by Usborne Publishing Limited, 20 Garrick Street, London WC2

# Part 1 Wild Flowers

This section of the book contains an identification guide to some of the wild flowers of Britain and Europe. The flowers are arranged by colour to make it easy for you to look them up.

The pictures in circles next to the main illustrations show close-ups of flowers or sometimes the fruits or seeds of the plant. These will help you to identify the flowers at different times of year.

For example, this Rosebay Willowherb appears in the section of the book that shows pink flowers. The picture in the circle below shows a close-up of a seed from this plant.

Seed of Rosebay
Willowherb
(seeds can be seen
after the plant has
finished flowering)

Top of
plant

The height
is given in
centimetres
(cm)

Rosebay
Willowherb

Ground
Level

The description next to each flower will also help you to identify it. The plants are not drawn to scale but the description gives you their average height measured from the ground. The last line of the description tells you the months when you usually see each plant in flower.

Beside the description is a small blank circle. Each time you spot a flower, make a tick like this in the correct circle.

## Areas Covered by this Book

The green area on this map shows the countries covered by this book. Not all the flowers that grow in these areas appear in the book. Some of the flowers shown are very rare in Britain, or do not grow here at all, but are common in other countries of Europe. Try to spot them if you go on holiday abroad.

## Scorecard

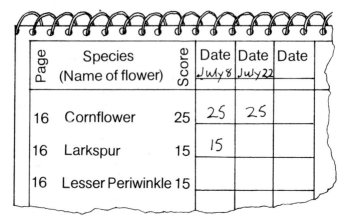

| Page | Species (Name of flower) | Score | Date July 8 | Date July 22 | Date |
|------|--------------------------|-------|-------------|--------------|------|
| 16 | Cornflower | 25 | 25 | 25 | |
| 16 | Larkspur | 15 | 15 | | |
| 16 | Lesser Periwinkle | 15 | | | |
| | | | | | |

The scorecard at the end of the book gives you a score for each flower you spot. A common flower scores 5 points, and a very rare one is worth 25 points. If you like, you can add up your score after a day out spotting. As some of the flowers are very difficult to find in the wild, you can tick off rare flowers if you see them on television or in a film.

**Notebook and pencils**

**Tape measure**

**Camera**

**Magnifying glass**

**Red Helleborine**

## What to Take

When you go out to spot flowers, take this book, a notebook and pencils with you so that you can record your finds. Take a tape measure to measure the height of plants and the length of runners. A magnifying glass will help you to take a closer look at the parts of flower heads. It is also useful for examining insects you may see on plants. Take a camera, if you have one, to photograph flowers (see page 58). Remember to make notes about the flowers you photograph.

Draw flowers you spot and note down details about them. Be sure to include the height of the plant, the colour and shape of the flower head and the leaves, and the place where the plant grows. If you find a flower that is not in this book, your drawing will help you to identify it from other books later. There is a list of useful books on page 59.

## Protecting Wild Flowers

Be careful not to tread on young plants or to break their stems.

Many wild plants that were once common are now rare, because people have picked and dug up so many. It is now against the law to dig up any wild plant by the roots, or to pick certain rare plants such as the Red Helleborine. If you pick wild flowers, they will die. Leave them for others to enjoy. It is much better to draw or photograph flowers, so that you and other people can see them again.

If you think you have found a rare plant, let your local nature conservation club know about it as soon as you can, so they can help protect it. You can get their address from your local library or Town Hall.

These pictures show the different parts of plants, and explain some of the words that appear in the book. When you are examining a plant, look closely at the flower head and the leaves. These will help you to identify it.

## Flowers

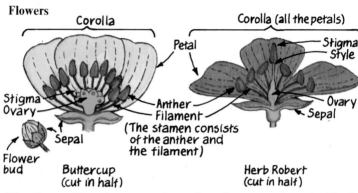

Corolla

Corolla (all the petals)

Petal

Stigma
Style

Stigma
Ovary

Anther
Filament
(The stamen consists
of the anther and
the filament)

Ovary

Sepal

Flower
bud

Sepal

Buttercup
(cut in half)

Herb Robert
(cut in half)

The stigma, style and ovary are the female parts of the flower, and the stamens are the male parts. Pollen from the stamens is received by the stigma. It causes seeds to grow inside the ovary.

The petals of some flowers are joined together.

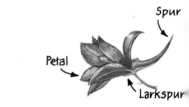

Corolla

Lily of the Valley

The petals of some flowers form a tube called a spur.

Spur

Petal

Larkspur

## Fruits and Seeds

The seeds of a plant are usually surrounded by the fruit. Fruits of different plants are of different sizes and shapes. They usually appear after the petals have withered and fallen off. Here are two examples.

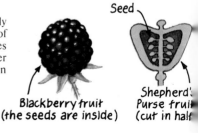

Seed

Blackberry fruit
(the seeds are inside)

Shepherd's
Purse fruit
(cut in half)

6

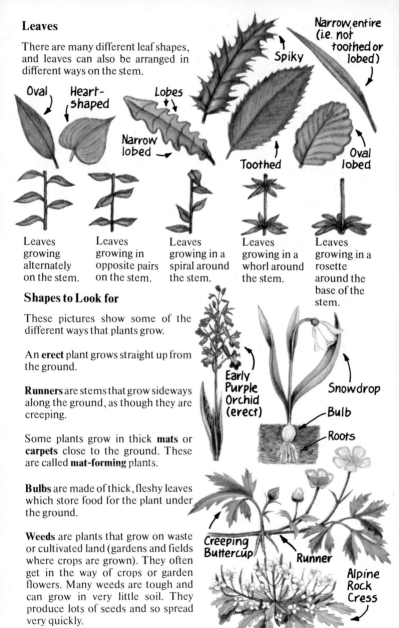

## Leaves

There are many different leaf shapes, and leaves can also be arranged in different ways on the stem.

Oval

Heart-shaped

Lobes

Narrow lobed

Spiky

Narrow, entire (i.e. not toothed or lobed)

Toothed

Oval lobed

Leaves growing alternately on the stem.

Leaves growing in opposite pairs on the stem.

Leaves growing in a spiral around the stem.

Leaves growing in a whorl around the stem.

Leaves growing in a rosette around the base of the stem.

## Shapes to Look for

These pictures show some of the different ways that plants grow.

An **erect** plant grows straight up from the ground.

**Runners** are stems that grow sideways along the ground, as though they are creeping.

Some plants grow in thick **mats** or **carpets** close to the ground. These are called **mat-forming** plants.

**Bulbs** are made of thick, fleshy leaves which store food for the plant under the ground.

**Weeds** are plants that grow on waste or cultivated land (gardens and fields where crops are grown). They often get in the way of crops or garden flowers. Many weeds are tough and can grow in very little soil. They produce lots of seeds and so spread very quickly.

Early Purple Orchid (erect)

Snowdrop

Bulb

Roots

Creeping Buttercup

Runner

Alpine Rock Cress

(mat-forming)

7

Look for these flowers in damp places, such as ditches, marshes and water meadows.

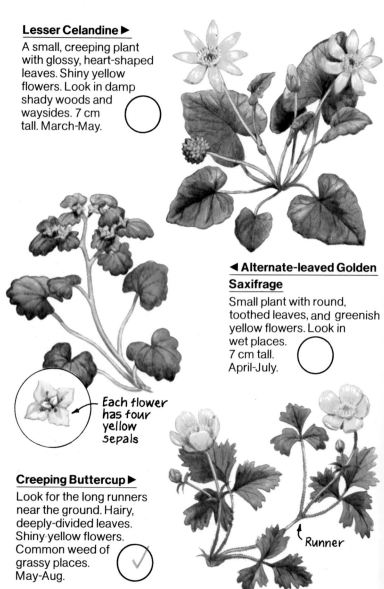

### Lesser Celandine ▶

A small, creeping plant with glossy, heart-shaped leaves. Shiny yellow flowers. Look in damp shady woods and waysides. 7 cm tall. March-May.

### ◀ Alternate-leaved Golden Saxifrage

Small plant with round, toothed leaves, and greenish yellow flowers. Look in wet places. 7 cm tall. April-July.

Each flower has four yellow sepals

### Creeping Buttercup ▶

Look for the long runners near the ground. Hairy, deeply-divided leaves. Shiny yellow flowers. Common weed of grassy places. May-Aug.

Runner

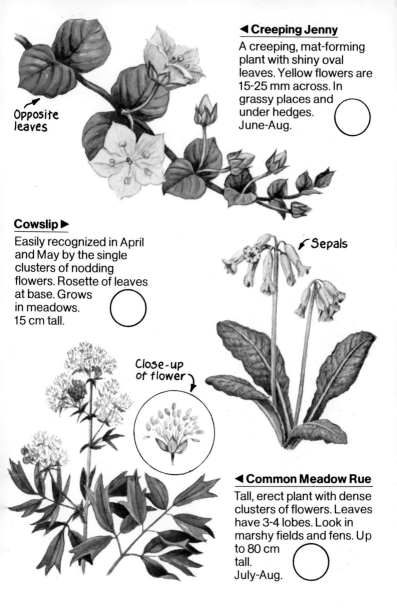

### ◀ Creeping Jenny

A creeping, mat-forming plant with shiny oval leaves. Yellow flowers are 15-25 mm across. In grassy places and under hedges. June-Aug.

Opposite leaves

### Cowslip ▶

Easily recognized in April and May by the single clusters of nodding flowers. Rosette of leaves at base. Grows in meadows. 15 cm tall.

Sepals

Close-up of flower

### ◀ Common Meadow Rue

Tall, erect plant with dense clusters of flowers. Leaves have 3-4 lobes. Look in marshy fields and fens. Up to 80 cm tall. July-Aug.

Look for these flowers, and those on page 11, in woods, hedgerows and heaths.

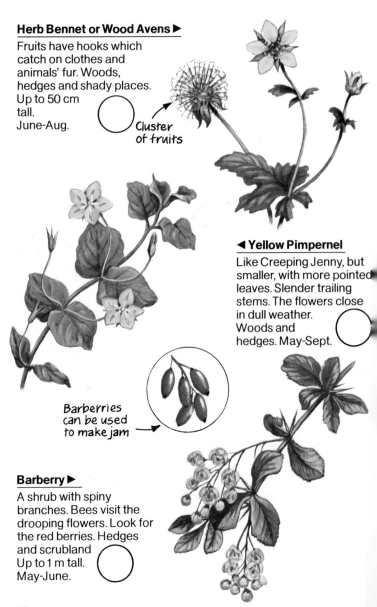

**Herb Bennet or Wood Avens ▶**

Fruits have hooks which catch on clothes and animals' fur. Woods, hedges and shady places. Up to 50 cm tall. June-Aug.

Cluster of fruits

**◀ Yellow Pimpernel**

Like Creeping Jenny, but smaller, with more pointed leaves. Slender trailing stems. The flowers close in dull weather. Woods and hedges. May-Sept.

Barberries can be used to make jam →

**Barberry ▶**

A shrub with spiny branches. Bees visit the drooping flowers. Look for the red berries. Hedges and scrubland Up to 1 m tall. May-June.

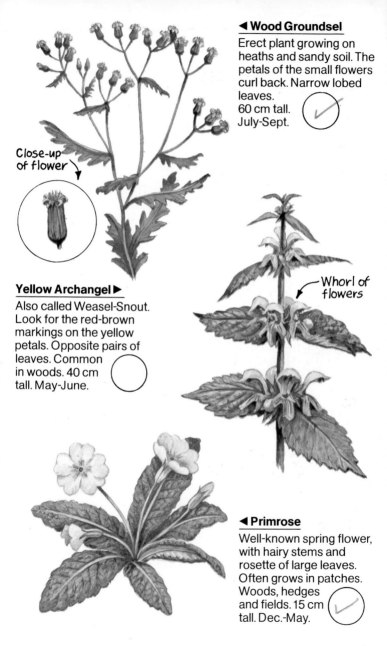

## ◀ Wood Groundsel

Erect plant growing on heaths and sandy soil. The petals of the small flowers curl back. Narrow lobed leaves.
60 cm tall.
July-Sept.

Close-up of flower

## Yellow Archangel ▶

Also called Weasel-Snout. Look for the red-brown markings on the yellow petals. Opposite pairs of leaves. Common in woods. 40 cm tall. May-June.

Whorl of flowers

## ◀ Primrose

Well-known spring flower, with hairy stems and rosette of large leaves. Often grows in patches. Woods, hedges and fields. 15 cm tall. Dec.-May.

Look for these flowers, and those on page 13, in open grassy places, such as heaths and commons.

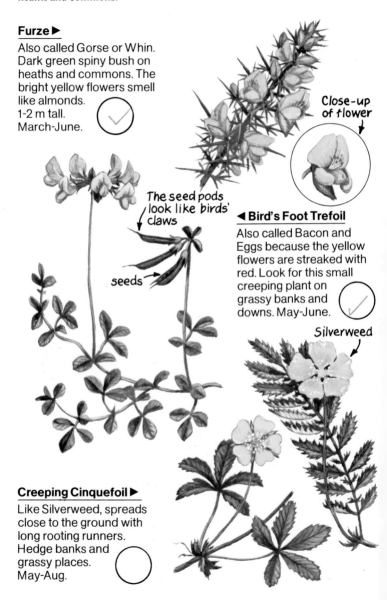

### Furze ▶
Also called Gorse or Whin. Dark green spiny bush on heaths and commons. The bright yellow flowers smell like almonds.
1-2 m tall.
March-June.

Close-up of flower

The seed pods look like birds' claws

seeds

### ◀ Bird's Foot Trefoil
Also called Bacon and Eggs because the yellow flowers are streaked with red. Look for this small creeping plant on grassy banks and downs. May-June.

Silverweed

### Creeping Cinquefoil ▶
Like Silverweed, spreads close to the ground with long rooting runners. Hedge banks and grassy places.
May-Aug.

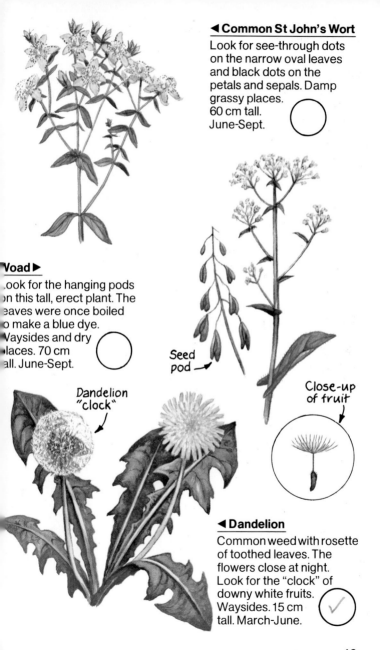

### ◀ Common St John's Wort

Look for see-through dots on the narrow oval leaves and black dots on the petals and sepals. Damp grassy places.
60 cm tall.
June-Sept.

### Woad ▶

Look for the hanging pods on this tall, erect plant. The leaves were once boiled to make a blue dye. Waysides and dry places. 70 cm tall. June-Sept.

Seed pod →

Close-up of fruit →

Dandelion "clock"

### ◀ Dandelion

Common weed with rosette of toothed leaves. The flowers close at night. Look for the "clock" of downy white fruits. Waysides. 15 cm tall. March-June.

### Stonecrop ▶

Also called Wallpepper.
Mat-forming plant with
star-shaped flowers. The
thick fleshy leaves have
a peppery taste.
Dunes, shingle and
walls. June-July.

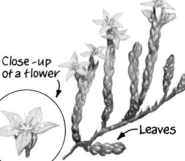

Close-up of a flower

Leaves

### ◀ Purslane

A low spreading plant with
red stems. The fleshy oval
shaped leaves are in
opposite pairs. A weed of
fields and waste
places.
May-Oct.

Close-up of a flower

### Golden Rod ▶

Erect plant with flowers on
thin spikes. Leaves are
narrower and more pointed
near top of plant. Woods,
banks and cliffs.
40 cm tall.
July-Sept.

Leaves
broader
near bottom
of plant

14

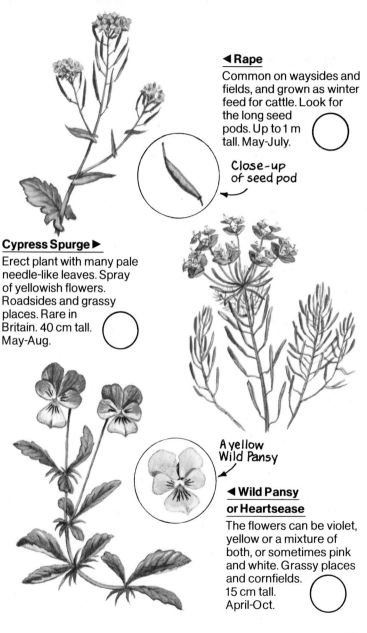

### ◀ Rape

Common on waysides and fields, and grown as winter feed for cattle. Look for the long seed pods. Up to 1 m tall. May-July.

Close-up of seed pod

### Cypress Spurge ▶

Erect plant with many pale needle-like leaves. Spray of yellowish flowers. Roadsides and grassy places. Rare in Britain. 40 cm tall. May-Aug.

A yellow Wild Pansy

### ◀ Wild Pansy or Heartsease

The flowers can be violet, yellow or a mixture of both, or sometimes pink and white. Grassy places and cornfields. 15 cm tall. April-Oct.

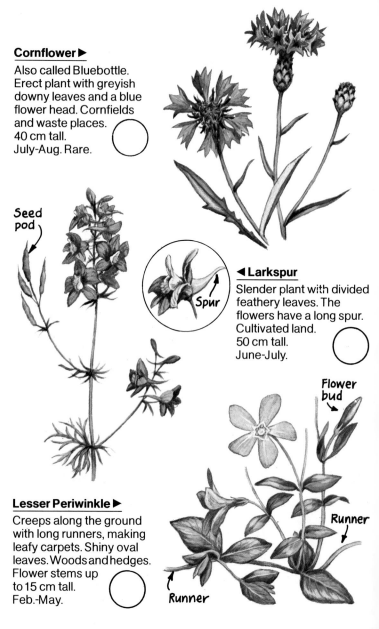

### Cornflower ▶

Also called Bluebottle.
Erect plant with greyish
downy leaves and a blue
flower head. Cornfields
and waste places.
40 cm tall.
July-Aug. Rare.

Seed
pod

Spur

### ◀ Larkspur

Slender plant with divided
feathery leaves. The
flowers have a long spur.
Cultivated land.
50 cm tall.
June-July.

Flower
bud

### Lesser Periwinkle ▶

Creeps along the ground
with long runners, making
leafy carpets. Shiny oval
leaves. Woods and hedges.
Flower stems up
to 15 cm tall.
Feb.-May.

Runner

Runner

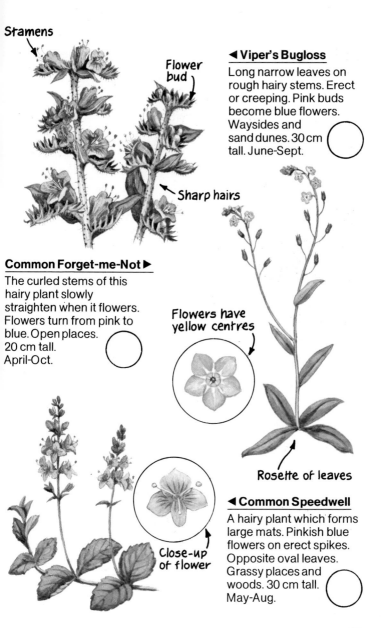

**Stamens**

**Flower bud**

**◄ Viper's Bugloss**

Long narrow leaves on rough hairy stems. Erect or creeping. Pink buds become blue flowers. Waysides and sand dunes. 30 cm tall. June-Sept.

**Sharp hairs**

**Common Forget-me-Not ►**

The curled stems of this hairy plant slowly straighten when it flowers. Flowers turn from pink to blue. Open places. 20 cm tall. April-Oct.

**Flowers have yellow centres**

**Rosette of leaves**

**Close-up of flower**

**◄ Common Speedwell**

A hairy plant which forms large mats. Pinkish blue flowers on erect spikes. Opposite oval leaves. Grassy places and woods. 30 cm tall. May-Aug.

Look for the flowers shown on this page in damp places.

## Common Monkshood ▶

Also called Wolfsbane. Notice hood on flowers and the deeply-divided leaves. Near streams and in damp woods. 70 cm tall. June-Sept.

Flower is shaped like a monk's hood

### ◀ Brooklime

Creeping plant with erect reddish stems. Shiny oval leaves in opposite pairs. Used to be eaten in salads. Wet places. 30 cm tall. May-Sept.

## Bugle ▶

Creeping plant with erect flower spikes. Purplish stem is hairy on two sides. Forms carpets in damp woods. 10-20 cm tall. May-June.

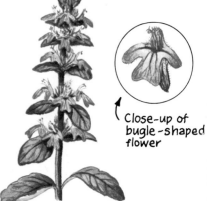

Close-up of bugle-shaped flower

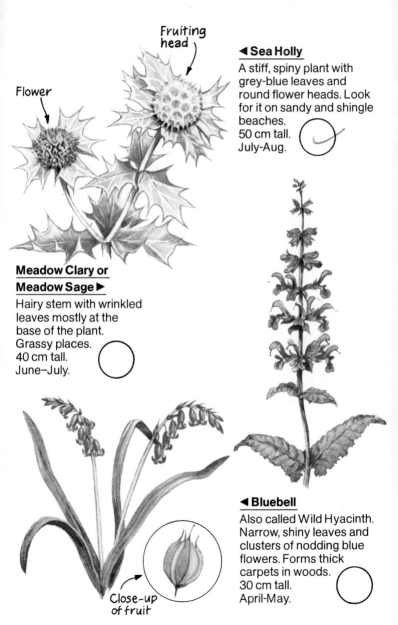

Fruiting head

Flower

**◄ Sea Holly**

A stiff, spiny plant with grey-blue leaves and round flower heads. Look for it on sandy and shingle beaches.
50 cm tall.
July-Aug.

**Meadow Clary or
Meadow Sage ►**

Hairy stem with wrinkled leaves mostly at the base of the plant. Grassy places.
40 cm tall.
June–July.

Close-up of fruit

**◄ Bluebell**

Also called Wild Hyacinth. Narrow, shiny leaves and clusters of nodding blue flowers. Forms thick carpets in woods.
30 cm tall.
April-May.

**19**

Look for the flowers shown on this page in woods or hedges.

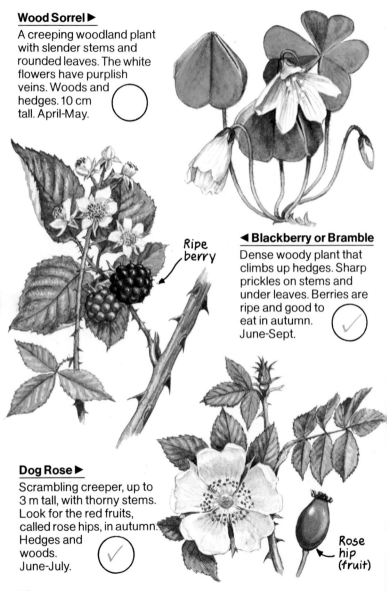

### Wood Sorrel ▶

A creeping woodland plant with slender stems and rounded leaves. The white flowers have purplish veins. Woods and hedges. 10 cm tall. April-May.

Ripe berry

### ◀ Blackberry or Bramble

Dense woody plant that climbs up hedges. Sharp prickles on stems and under leaves. Berries are ripe and good to eat in autumn. June-Sept.

### Dog Rose ▶

Scrambling creeper, up to 3 m tall, with thorny stems. Look for the red fruits, called rose hips, in autumn. Hedges and woods. June-July.

Rose hip (fruit)

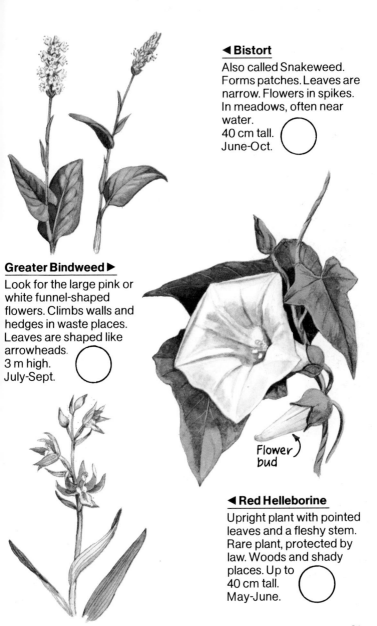

### ◀ Bistort

Also called Snakeweed.
Forms patches. Leaves are
narrow. Flowers in spikes.
In meadows, often near
water.
40 cm tall.
June-Oct.

### Greater Bindweed ▶

Look for the large pink or
white funnel-shaped
flowers. Climbs walls and
hedges in waste places.
Leaves are shaped like
arrowheads.
3 m high.
July-Sept.

Flower
bud

### ◀ Red Helleborine

Upright plant with pointed
leaves and a fleshy stem.
Rare plant, protected by
law. Woods and shady
places. Up to
40 cm tall.
May-June.

21

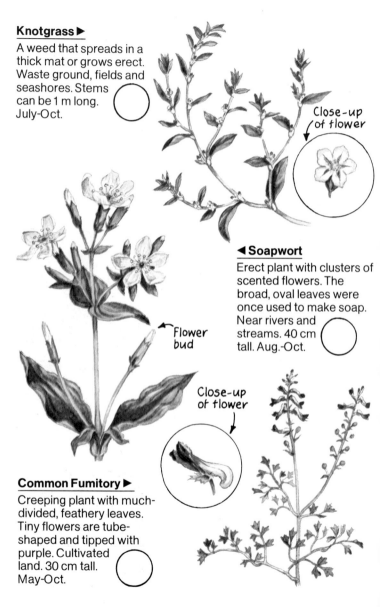

### Knotgrass ▶
A weed that spreads in a thick mat or grows erect. Waste ground, fields and seashores. Stems can be 1 m long. July-Oct.

Close-up of flower

### ◀ Soapwort
Erect plant with clusters of scented flowers. The broad, oval leaves were once used to make soap. Near rivers and streams. 40 cm tall. Aug.-Oct.

Flower bud

Close-up of flower

### Common Fumitory ▶
Creeping plant with much-divided, feathery leaves. Tiny flowers are tube-shaped and tipped with purple. Cultivated land. 30 cm tall. May-Oct.

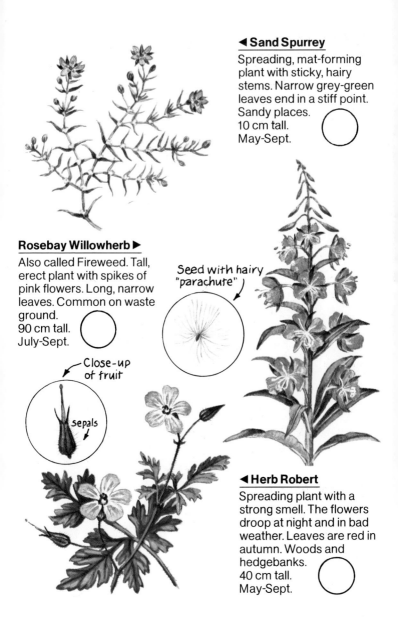

### ◀ Sand Spurrey

Spreading, mat-forming plant with sticky, hairy stems. Narrow grey-green leaves end in a stiff point. Sandy places.
10 cm tall.
May-Sept.

### Rosebay Willowherb ▶

Also called Fireweed. Tall, erect plant with spikes of pink flowers. Long, narrow leaves. Common on waste ground.
90 cm tall.
July-Sept.

Seed with hairy "parachute"

Close-up of fruit

sepals

### ◀ Herb Robert

Spreading plant with a strong smell. The flowers droop at night and in bad weather. Leaves are red in autumn. Woods and hedgebanks.
40 cm tall.
May-Sept.

Look for these flowers on heaths and moors.

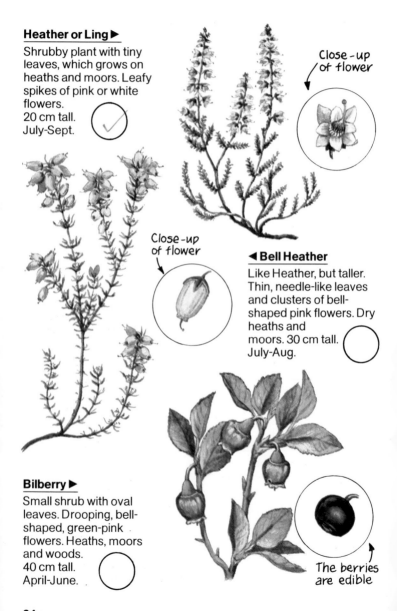

### Heather or Ling ▶

Shrubby plant with tiny leaves, which grows on heaths and moors. Leafy spikes of pink or white flowers.
20 cm tall.
July-Sept.

Close-up of flower

Close-up of flower

### ◀ Bell Heather

Like Heather, but taller. Thin, needle-like leaves and clusters of bell-shaped pink flowers. Dry heaths and moors. 30 cm tall. July-Aug.

### Bilberry ▶

Small shrub with oval leaves. Drooping, bell-shaped, green-pink flowers. Heaths, moors and woods.
40 cm tall.
April-June.

The berries are edible

Look for these flowers in dry, grassy places.

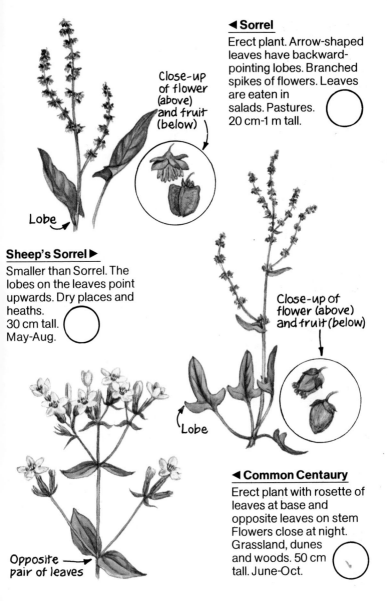

Close-up
of flower
(above)
and fruit
(below)

### ◀ Sorrel

Erect plant. Arrow-shaped leaves have backward-pointing lobes. Branched spikes of flowers. Leaves are eaten in salads. Pastures. 20 cm-1 m tall.

Lobe

### Sheep's Sorrel ▶

Smaller than Sorrel. The lobes on the leaves point upwards. Dry places and heaths.
30 cm tall.
May-Aug.

Close-up of
flower (above)
and fruit (below)

Lobe

### ◀ Common Centaury

Erect plant with rosette of leaves at base and opposite leaves on stem Flowers close at night. Grassland, dunes and woods. 50 cm tall. June-Oct.

Opposite
pair of leaves

### Ragged Robin ▶

Flowers have ragged pink petals. Erect plant with a forked stem and narrow, pointed leaves. Damp meadows, marshes and woods.
30-70 cm tall.
May-June.

— A bract is a kind of small leaf near the flower

Grooved stem

### ◀ Knapweed or Hard-head

Erect plant with brush-like pink flowers growing from black bracts. Grassland and waysides.
40 cm tall.
June-Sept.

### Hemp Agrimony ▶

Tough, erect plant with downy stem. Grows in patches in damp places. Attracts butterflies.
Up to 120 cm tall.
July–Sept.

Whorl of leaves

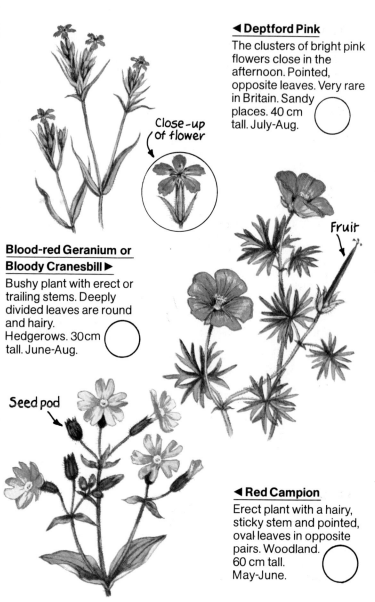

### ◄ Deptford Pink

The clusters of bright pink flowers close in the afternoon. Pointed, opposite leaves. Very rare in Britain. Sandy places. 40 cm tall. July-Aug.

Close-up of flower

### Blood-red Geranium or
### Bloody Cranesbill ►

Bushy plant with erect or trailing stems. Deeply divided leaves are round and hairy. Hedgerows. 30 cm tall. June-Aug.

Fruit

Seed pod

### ◄ Red Campion

Erect plant with a hairy, sticky stem and pointed, oval leaves in opposite pairs. Woodland. 60 cm tall. May-June.

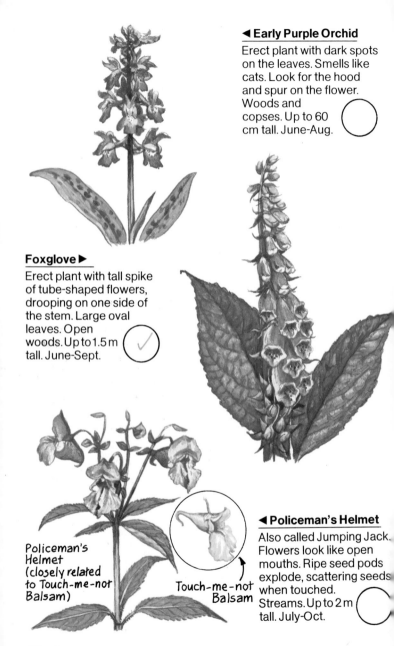

### ◄ Early Purple Orchid
Erect plant with dark spots on the leaves. Smells like cats. Look for the hood and spur on the flower. Woods and copses. Up to 60 cm tall. June-Aug.

### Foxglove ►
Erect plant with tall spike of tube-shaped flowers, drooping on one side of the stem. Large oval leaves. Open woods. Up to 1.5 m tall. June-Sept.

Policeman's Helmet (closely related to Touch-me-not Balsam)

Touch-me-not Balsam

### ◄ Policeman's Helmet
Also called Jumping Jack. Flowers look like open mouths. Ripe seed pods explode, scattering seeds when touched. Streams. Up to 2 m tall. July-Oct.

Look for the flowers shown on this page in woods or hedgerows.

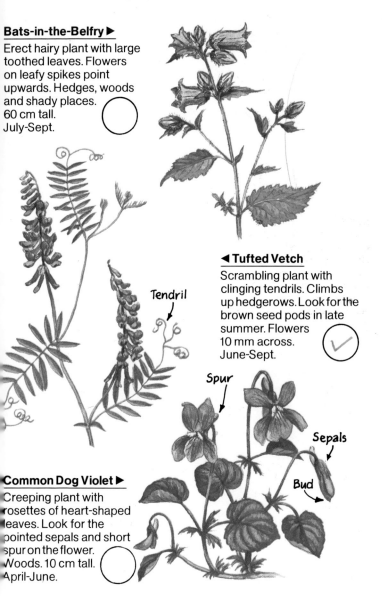

### Bats-in-the-Belfry ▶

Erect hairy plant with large
toothed leaves. Flowers
on leafy spikes point
upwards. Hedges, woods
and shady places.
60 cm tall.
July-Sept.

### ◀ Tufted Vetch

Scrambling plant with
clinging tendrils. Climbs
up hedgerows. Look for the
brown seed pods in late
summer. Flowers
10 mm across.
June-Sept.

Tendril

Spur

Sepals

Bud

### Common Dog Violet ▶

Creeping plant with
rosettes of heart-shaped
leaves. Look for the
pointed sepals and short
spur on the flower.
Woods. 10 cm tall.
April-June.

Look in fields and other grassy places for these flowers.

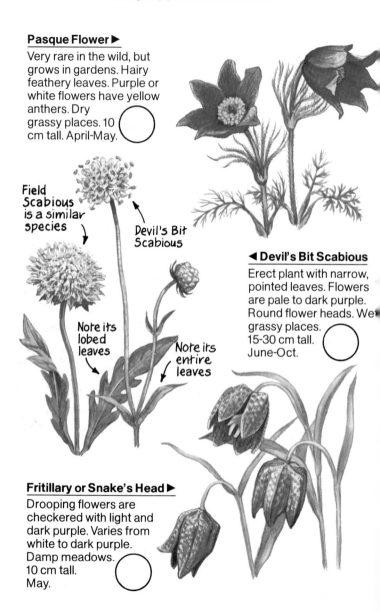

### Pasque Flower ▶
Very rare in the wild, but grows in gardens. Hairy feathery leaves. Purple or white flowers have yellow anthers. Dry grassy places. 10 cm tall. April-May.

Field Scabious is a similar species

Devil's Bit Scabious

Note its lobed leaves

Note its entire leaves

### ◀ Devil's Bit Scabious
Erect plant with narrow, pointed leaves. Flowers are pale to dark purple. Round flower heads. Wet grassy places. 15-30 cm tall. June-Oct.

### Fritillary or Snake's Head ▶
Drooping flowers are checkered with light and dark purple. Varies from white to dark purple. Damp meadows. 10 cm tall. May.

You may see these flowers on old walls.

Spur

### ◀ Ivy-leaved Toadflax
Weak, slender stalks trail on old walls. Look for the yellow lips on the mauve flowers. Flowers 10 mm across. Shiny, ivy-shaped leaves. May-Sept.

### Houseleek ▶
A rosette plant with thick fleshy leaves. Dull red spiky petals. Does not flower every year. Old walls and roofs. 30-60 cm tall. June-July.

Rosette of leaves

The stalk, with flowers, does not appear very often. Usually you will see only the rosette.

Fruits

### ◀ Snapdragon
Erect plant with spike of flowers. Long, narrow leaves. Pouch-like flowers are yellow inside. Old walls, rocks and gardens. 40 cm tall. June-Sept.

Look for these flowers on cultivated land.

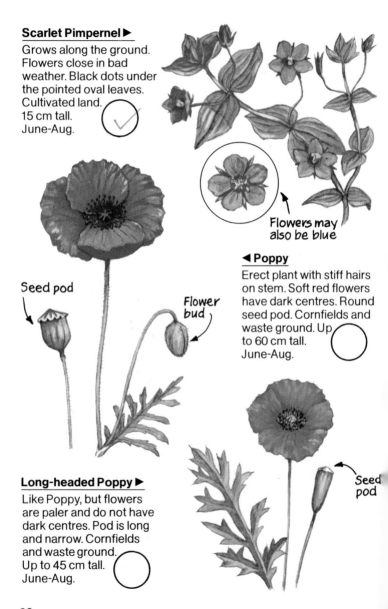

## Scarlet Pimpernel ▶

Grows along the ground.
Flowers close in bad
weather. Black dots under
the pointed oval leaves.
Cultivated land.
15 cm tall.
June-Aug.

Flowers may
also be blue

Seed pod

Flower
bud

## ◀ Poppy

Erect plant with stiff hairs
on stem. Soft red flowers
have dark centres. Round
seed pod. Cornfields and
waste ground. Up
to 60 cm tall.
June-Aug.

Seed
pod

## Long-headed Poppy ▶

Like Poppy, but flowers
are paler and do not have
dark centres. Pod is long
and narrow. Cornfields
and waste ground.
Up to 45 cm tall.
June-Aug.

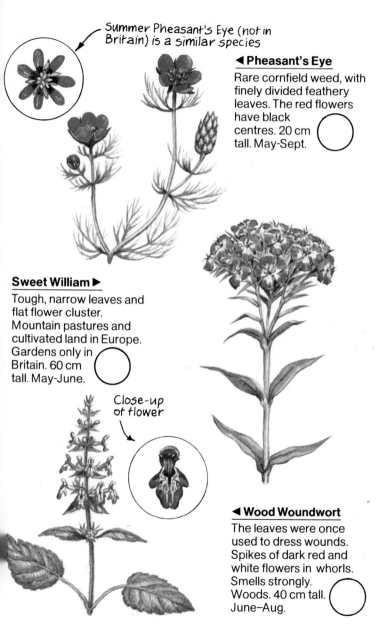

Summer Pheasant's Eye (not in Britain) is a similar species

### ◀ Pheasant's Eye

Rare cornfield weed, with finely divided feathery leaves. The red flowers have black centres. 20 cm tall. May-Sept.

### Sweet William ▶

Tough, narrow leaves and flat flower cluster. Mountain pastures and cultivated land in Europe. Gardens only in Britain. 60 cm tall. May-June.

Close-up of flower

### ◀ Wood Woundwort

The leaves were once used to dress wounds. Spikes of dark red and white flowers in whorls. Smells strongly. Woods. 40 cm tall. June–Aug.

The flowers on these two pages can be found in woodlands, quite early in the year.

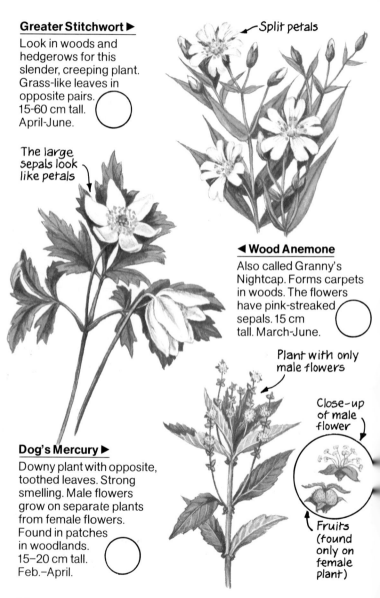

### Greater Stitchwort ▶

Look in woods and hedgerows for this slender, creeping plant. Grass-like leaves in opposite pairs. 15-60 cm tall. April-June.

Split petals

The large sepals look like petals

### ◀ Wood Anemone

Also called Granny's Nightcap. Forms carpets in woods. The flowers have pink-streaked sepals. 15 cm tall. March-June.

Plant with only male flowers

Close-up of male flower

### Dog's Mercury ▶

Downy plant with opposite, toothed leaves. Strong smelling. Male flowers grow on separate plants from female flowers. Found in patches in woodlands. 15–20 cm tall. Feb.–April.

Fruits (found only on female plant)

Notice the long veins that run from one end of the leaf to the other

### ◄ Ramsons or Wood Garlic

Smells of garlic. Broad, bright green leaves grow from a bulb. Forms carpets in damp woods, often with Bluebells.
10-25 cm tall.
April-June.

### Lily-of-the-Valley ►

Grows in dry woods. Broad, dark green leaves and sweet-smelling flowers. Red berries in summer. Also a garden plant. 20 cm tall. May-June.

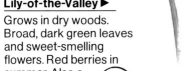

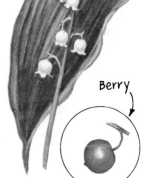

Berry

### ◄ Snowdrop

Welcomed as the first flower of the new year. Dark green, narrow leaves. Nodding white flowers. Woods.
20 cm tall.
Jan.-March.

Look for these flowers in hedges or woods.

### Jack-by-the-Hedge or Garlic Mustard ▶

Erect plant with heart-shaped, toothed leaves. Smells of garlic. Common in hedges. Up to 1.2 m tall. April-June.

Seed pods

Fruits are smaller than garden strawberries

### ◀ Wild Strawberry

Small plant with long, arching runners and oval, toothed leaves in threes. Sweet red fruits, covered with seeds. Woods and scrubland. April-July.

Tendril

### Wild Pea ▶

Very rare, scrambling plant with grey-green leaves. The seeds, or peas, are inside the pods. Climbs on thickets and hedges. Up to 2.5 m high. June-Aug.

Pod

Look for these flowers in hedges and waysides.

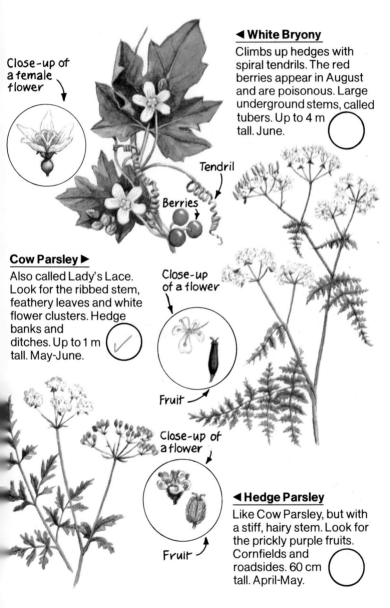

**◄ White Bryony**

Climbs up hedges with spiral tendrils. The red berries appear in August and are poisonous. Large underground stems, called tubers. Up to 4 m tall. June.

Close-up of a female flower

Tendril

Berries

**Cow Parsley ►**

Also called Lady's Lace. Look for the ribbed stem, feathery leaves and white flower clusters. Hedge banks and ditches. Up to 1 m tall. May-June.

Close-up of a flower

Fruit

Close-up of a flower

**◄ Hedge Parsley**

Like Cow Parsley, but with a stiff, hairy stem. Look for the prickly purple fruits. Cornfields and roadsides. 60 cm tall. April-May.

Fruit

These flowers can be found in or near fresh water (streams, ponds, etc.).

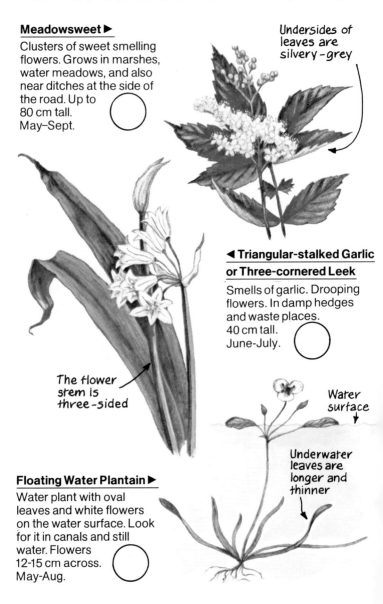

## Meadowsweet ▶

Clusters of sweet smelling flowers. Grows in marshes, water meadows, and also near ditches at the side of the road. Up to 80 cm tall.
May–Sept.

Undersides of leaves are silvery-grey

## ◀ Triangular-stalked Garlic or Three-cornered Leek

Smells of garlic. Drooping flowers. In damp hedges and waste places.
40 cm tall.
June-July.

The flower stem is three-sided

Water surface

Underwater leaves are longer and thinner

## Floating Water Plantain ▶

Water plant with oval leaves and white flowers on the water surface. Look for it in canals and still water. Flowers 12-15 cm across.
May-Aug.

These flowers can be found in or near fresh water (streams, ponds, etc.).

### ◀ Water Crowfoot
Water plant whose roots are anchored in the mud at the bottom of ponds and streams. Flowers (10–20 mm across) cover the water surface.
May–June.

Fine, underwater leaves

These leaves are on the water surface

### Water Soldier ▶
Under water except when it flowers. Long saw-like leaves then show above the surface. Flowers 30-40 mm across. Ponds, canals, ditches. June-Aug.

Bud

### ◀ Frogbit
Rises to the surface in spring, and spreads with long runners. Shiny round leaves grow in tufts. Flowers 20 mm across. Canals and ponds. July-Aug.

Runner

Look for these flowers in fields and other grassy places.

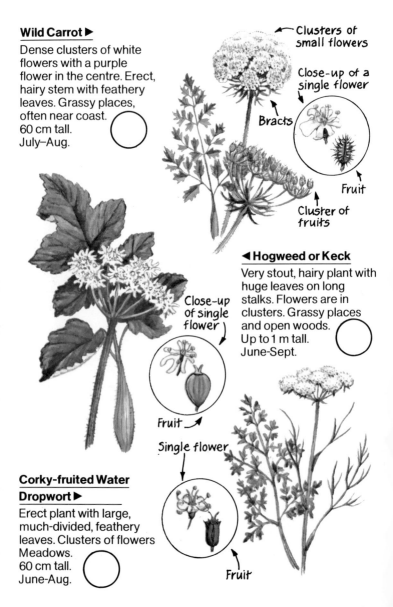

### Wild Carrot ▶

Dense clusters of white flowers with a purple flower in the centre. Erect, hairy stem with feathery leaves. Grassy places, often near coast.
60 cm tall.
July–Aug.

Clusters of small flowers

Close-up of a single flower

Bracts

Fruit

Cluster of fruits

### ◀ Hogweed or Keck

Very stout, hairy plant with huge leaves on long stalks. Flowers are in clusters. Grassy places and open woods.
Up to 1 m tall.
June-Sept.

Close-up of single flower

Fruit

### Corky-fruited Water Dropwort ▶

Erect plant with large, much-divided, feathery leaves. Clusters of flowers Meadows.
60 cm tall.
June-Aug.

Single flower

Fruit

Look for these flowers in fields and other grassy places.

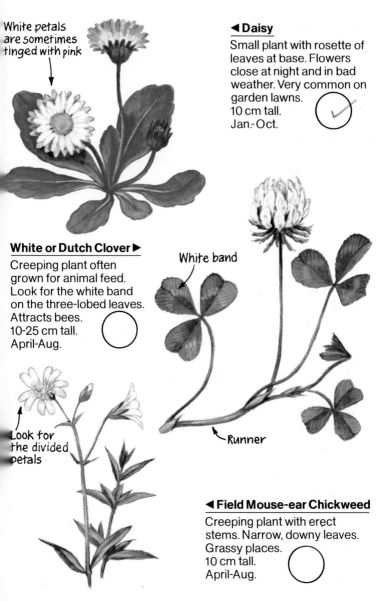

White petals are sometimes tinged with pink

### ◀ Daisy
Small plant with rosette of leaves at base. Flowers close at night and in bad weather. Very common on garden lawns.
10 cm tall.
Jan.-Oct.

### White or Dutch Clover ▶
Creeping plant often grown for animal feed. Look for the white band on the three-lobed leaves. Attracts bees.
10-25 cm tall.
April-Aug.

White band

Runner

Look for the divided petals

### ◀ Field Mouse-ear Chickweed
Creeping plant with erect stems. Narrow, downy leaves. Grassy places.
10 cm tall.
April-Aug.

Look for these flowers on cultivated land, waste land and waysides.

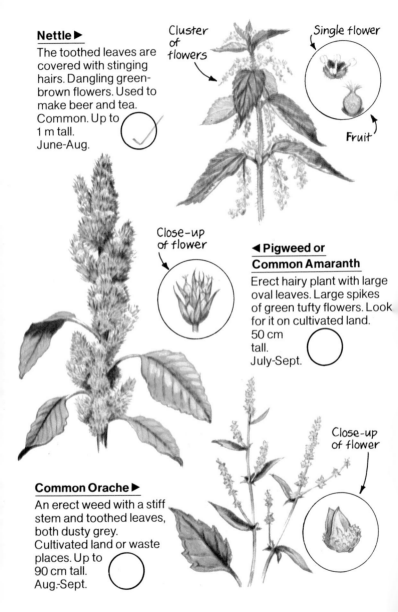

### Nettle ▶
The toothed leaves are covered with stinging hairs. Dangling green-brown flowers. Used to make beer and tea. Common. Up to 1 m tall. June-Aug.

Cluster of flowers

Single flower

Fruit

Close-up of flower

### ◀ Pigweed or Common Amaranth
Erect hairy plant with large oval leaves. Large spikes of green tufty flowers. Look for it on cultivated land. 50 cm tall. July-Sept.

Close-up of flower

### Common Orache ▶
An erect weed with a stiff stem and toothed leaves, both dusty grey. Cultivated land or waste places. Up to 90 cm tall. Aug.-Sept.

Look for these flowers on cultivated land, waste land and waysides.

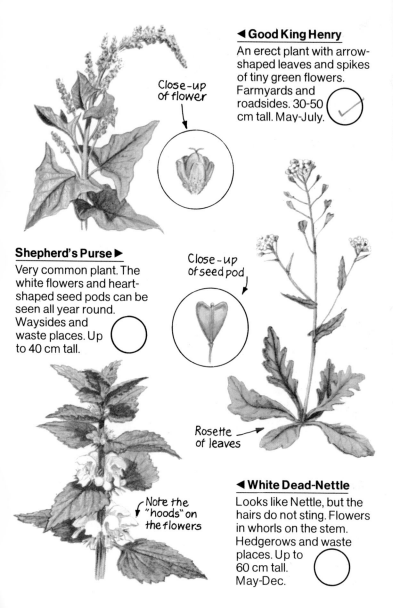

### ◀ Good King Henry

An erect plant with arrow-shaped leaves and spikes of tiny green flowers. Farmyards and roadsides. 30-50 cm tall. May-July.

Close-up of flower

### Shepherd's Purse ▶

Very common plant. The white flowers and heart-shaped seed pods can be seen all year round. Waysides and waste places. Up to 40 cm tall.

Close-up of seed pod

Rosette of leaves

Note the "hoods" on the flowers

### ◀ White Dead-Nettle

Looks like Nettle, but the hairs do not sting. Flowers in whorls on the stem. Hedgerows and waste places. Up to 60 cm tall. May-Dec.

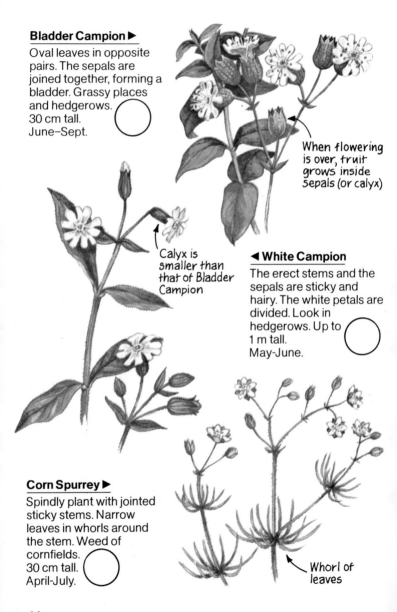

### Bladder Campion ▶

Oval leaves in opposite pairs. The sepals are joined together, forming a bladder. Grassy places and hedgerows. 30 cm tall. June–Sept.

When flowering is over, fruit grows inside sepals (or calyx)

Calyx is smaller than that of Bladder Campion

### ◀ White Campion

The erect stems and the sepals are sticky and hairy. The white petals are divided. Look in hedgerows. Up to 1 m tall. May-June.

### Corn Spurrey ▶

Spindly plant with jointed sticky stems. Narrow leaves in whorls around the stem. Weed of cornfields. 30 cm tall. April-July.

Whorl of leaves

### ◀ Chickweed

Mat-forming plant with stems that can grow up to 40 cm tall. You can see the small flowers all year round. Common weed in fields, gardens.

### Black Nightshade ▶

Shrubby weed of cultivated ground. Shiny oval leaves. Petals fold back to show yellow anthers. The berries are poisonous. 20 cm tall. July-Sept.

Anthers

Berries

Whorl of leaves

Fruit

### ◀ Goosegrass or Common Cleavers

Scrambling plant. The prickly stems stick to clothes and animal fur. Hedges. 60 cm tall. June-Sept.

Look for these flowers in grassy places, on waste or cultivated ground.

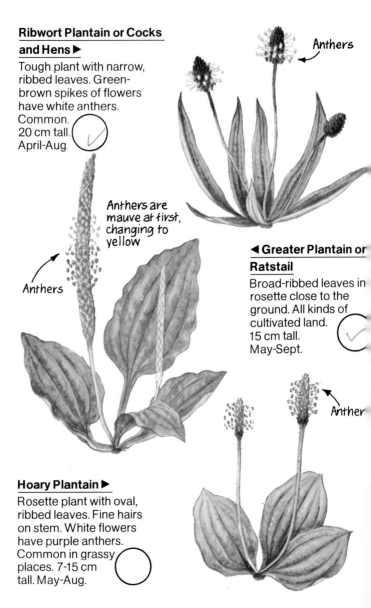

### Ribwort Plantain or Cocks and Hens ▶

Tough plant with narrow, ribbed leaves. Green-brown spikes of flowers have white anthers. Common. 20 cm tall. April-Aug.

Anthers

Anthers are mauve at first, changing to yellow

Anthers

### ◀ Greater Plantain or Ratstail

Broad-ribbed leaves in rosette close to the ground. All kinds of cultivated land. 15 cm tall. May-Sept.

Anther

### Hoary Plantain ▶

Rosette plant with oval, ribbed leaves. Fine hairs on stem. White flowers have purple anthers. Common in grassy places. 7-15 cm tall. May-Aug.

Look for these flowers on grassy or waste ground.

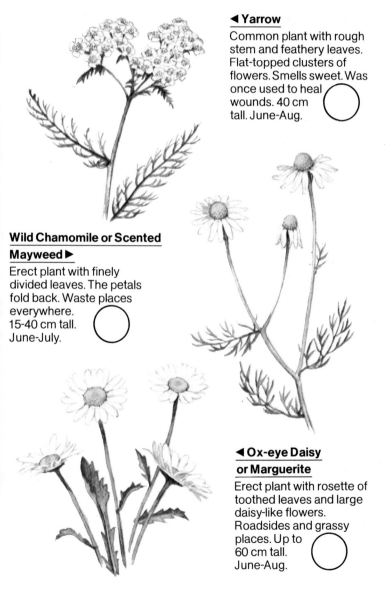

### ◀ Yarrow
Common plant with rough stem and feathery leaves. Flat-topped clusters of flowers. Smells sweet. Was once used to heal wounds. 40 cm tall. June-Aug.

### Wild Chamomile or Scented Mayweed ▶
Erect plant with finely divided leaves. The petals fold back. Waste places everywhere. 15-40 cm tall. June-July.

### ◀ Ox-eye Daisy or Marguerite
Erect plant with rosette of toothed leaves and large daisy-like flowers. Roadsides and grassy places. Up to 60 cm tall. June-Aug.

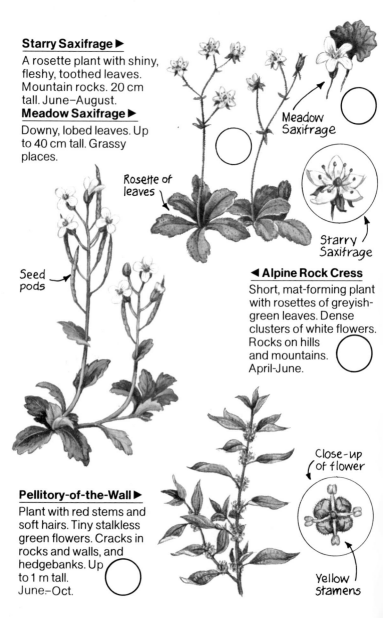

### Starry Saxifrage ▶

A rosette plant with shiny, fleshy, toothed leaves. Mountain rocks. 20 cm tall. June–August.

### Meadow Saxifrage ▶

Downy, lobed leaves. Up to 40 cm tall. Grassy places.

Meadow Saxifrage

Rosette of leaves

Starry Saxifrage

Seed pods

### ◀ Alpine Rock Cress

Short, mat-forming plant with rosettes of greyish-green leaves. Dense clusters of white flowers. Rocks on hills and mountains. April-June.

### Pellitory-of-the-Wall ▶

Plant with red stems and soft hairs. Tiny stalkless green flowers. Cracks in rocks and walls, and hedgebanks. Up to 1 m tall. June–Oct.

Close-up of flower

Yellow stamens

# Trick Picture Puzzle

These trick pictures show only parts of some of the plants that appear in this book. Can you guess what they are? The answers are upside-down at the bottom of the page.

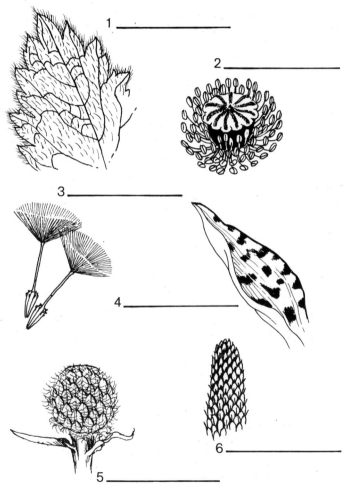

1 _____

2 _____

3 _____

4 _____

5 _____

6 _____

1. Nettle leaf 2. Stigma and stamens of Poppy 3. Dandelion fruits 4. Leaf of Early Purple Orchid 5. Knapweed bud 6. Flower tip of Greater Plantain.

# Colouring Quiz

These pictures show outlines of some of the flowers that appear in the book. Can you name them from their shapes and colour them correctly? Their names are upside-down at the bottom of the opposite page.

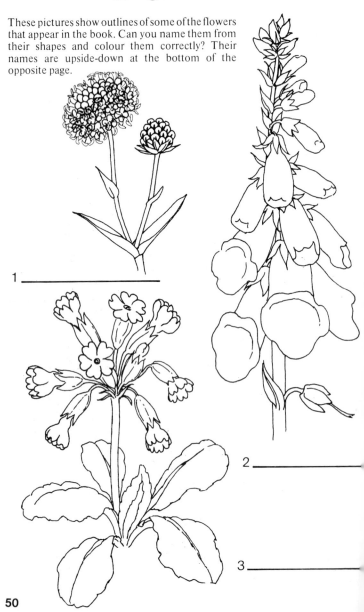

1 _____

2 _____

3 _____

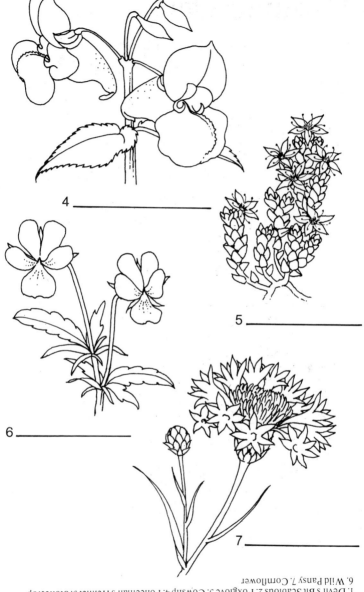

4 _____

5 _____

6 _____

7 _____

1. Devil's Bit Scabious 2. Foxglove 3. Cowslip 4. Policeman's Helmet 5. Stonecrop 6. Wild Pansy 7. Cornflower

# Find the Fruits

The pictures in the middle of these pages show fruits from the same plants as the flowers on these pages. Can you match each fruit with its correct flower? The answers are upside-down at the bottom of the opposite page.

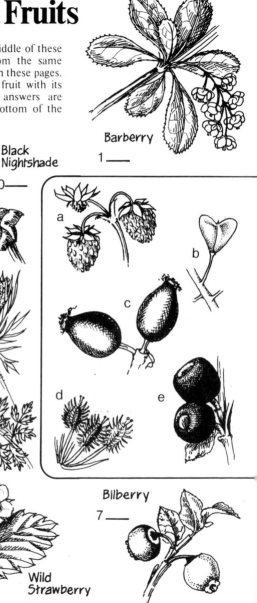

Barberry
1 ___

Black Nightshade
10 ___

Wild Carrot
9 ___

Bilberry
7 ___

Wild Strawberry
8 ___

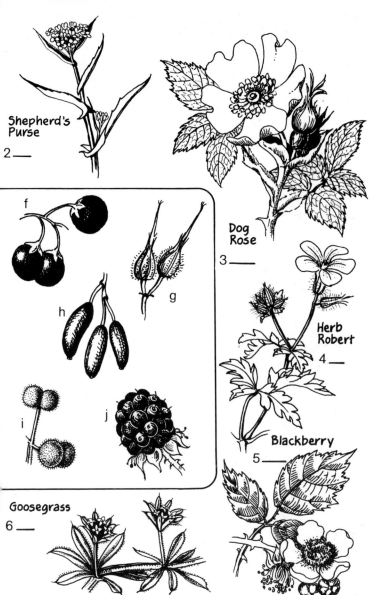

Shepherd's Purse

2 ___

f

h

g

Dog Rose

3 ___

Herb Robert

4 ___

Blackberry

5 ___

i

j

Goosegrass

6 ___

1i: Barberry 2b: Shepherd's Purse 3c: Dog Rose 4g: Herb Robert 5j: Blackberry
6i: Goosegrass 7e: Bilberry 8a: Wild Strawberry 9d: Wild Carrot 10f: Black Nightshade

53

# Where do they Grow?

The pictures in the middle of these pages show four places where wild flowers grow. Can you write the correct letter beside each flower's name to show where each one lives? The answers are upside-down at the bottom of the opposite page.

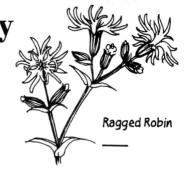

Ragged Robin
____

Houseleek
____

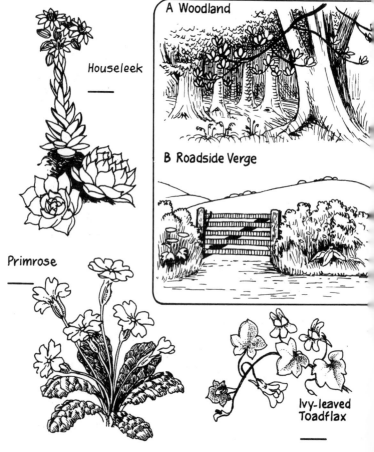

A Woodland

B Roadside Verge

Primrose
____

Ivy-leaved Toadflax
____

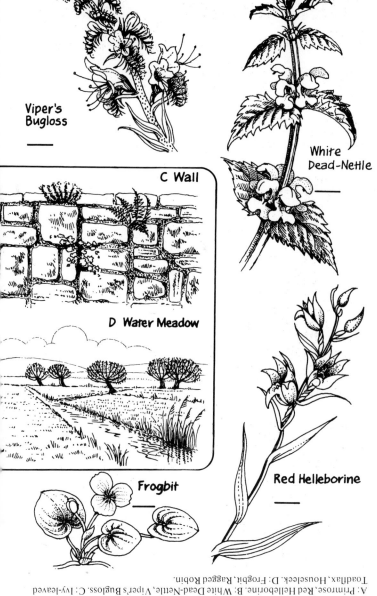

Viper's Bugloss
___

White Dead-Nettle
___

C Wall

D Water Meadow

Frogbit
___

Red Helleborine
___

A: Primrose. Red Helleborine. B: White Dead-Nettle. Viper's Bugloss. C: Ivy-leaved Toadflax, Houseleek. D: Frogbit. Ragged Robin.

55

# Make a Flower Notebook

Choose a spot near your home to study plants that grow there. If you live in the country, find a wide, grassy roadside verge or a disused railway cutting for your study.

If you are in a town, choose an empty garden, a churchyard or a grassy bank beside a canal. These are all areas where plants have had a long time to grow undisturbed, so you will be able to find many different kinds.

Mark out about a square metre of ground with sticks and string. Count and identify the flowers growing there and measure their height. Note how many of the same plants you see.

Try to find out why they grow in the same area. You could choose and mark out another study area where different plants grow and compare the ones you find with those in your other area.

Look carefully at the picture below. It shows a study area marked out on a grassy bank. Can you identify the plants growing there? They are Daisy, Nettle, Red Campion, Larkspur, Greater Plantain, Bird's Foot Trefoil and Dandelion.

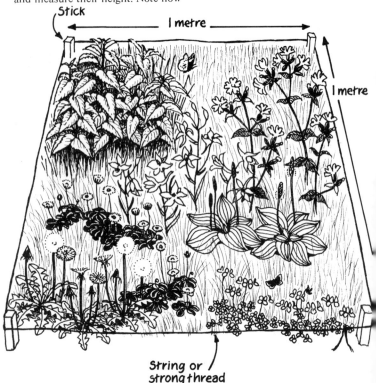

Stick

I metre

I metre

String or strong thread

Make a notebook to record changes in the flowers you find throughout the year. Use a loose-leaf binder or an exercise book. Draw only one plant on a page and write down where you found it.

You can also pick very common flowers and press them, to illustrate your book. Put the flower between two pieces of blotting paper and rest some heavy books on it. When it is dry, carefully stick it into your book with a spot of glue.

On the opposite page, make a chart and note changes in the appearance of the plant in different seasons. If a new plant starts to grow in your study area, make a page for it. Look out, too, for butterflies and other insects. Note which plants they feed on and look for butterfly eggs on the leaves.

COW PARSLEY

found on grass verge by hedge

| Date | Weather | Height | Remarks |
|------|---------|--------|---------|
| May 6 | Sunny | 60 cm | Flowering |
| May 17 | cloudy | 61 cm | Ladybird on stem |

# Photographing Flowers

Photographs make a good record of the flowers you spot. Stick your photos into an album, label them, and write notes about where you spotted the flowers, their height, and other details. Cut photographs of flowers out of magazines and add them to your collection.

Here are some tips to help you to take successful photographs.

Use a colour film. Always take photographs with the sun behind you and make sure that your shadow does not fall on the flower. Try to photograph the whole plant so that the stem and leaves are visible.

With a simple camera, you cannot photograph flowers in close-up, so choose your flower carefully. Tiny flowers photographed from a distance will not show up at all. A tall plant with large flowers or a patch of creeping plants will make good photographs.

If you lie flat on the ground and photograph a flower from below, outlined against the sky, it will stand out clearly. Sunlight filtering through the leaves shows up the veins in them.

To prevent a flower from being lost among grass and leaves, you can prop a piece of black or coloured card behind it and photograph it against this background.

If you want to photograph flowers in a wood, where the light is dim, experiment with a flash cube.

Be sure to make notes about the flowers when you photograph them. Refer to these notes when you are writing in your photo album.

Sea Pink
Portland
on cliffs
16 May 1977
Height 12cm
also on beach

Marsh Mallow
beside River Frome
Aug 27  Height 1m

Corn marigold
edge of barley field
Loders Farm, Cerne
24 June Height 30cm

Wild Arum
Hedge banks in
Marshwood Vale
20 May Height 25cm

Primrose
Hatch Wood
4 April
Height 12cm

# Books to Read

*The Wild Flowers of Britain and Northern Europe.* R. Fitter, A. Fitter, M. Blamey (Collins). Easy to use, light to carry, cheap reference paperback.
*The Concise British Flora in Colour.* W. Keble Martin (Ebury Press/ Michael Joseph). Large book, good illustrations.
*The Concise Flowers of Europe.* O. Polunin (Oxford University Press). Photos and short descriptions.
*The Nature Trail Book of Wild Flowers.* S. Tarsky (Usborne). Cheap. How to study and record flowers. Lots of interesting ideas.

*Wild Flowers of the Spring.* G. E. Hyde (Warne).
*Wild Flowers of the Summer.* G. E. Hyde (Warne). Small, cheap, reference books with photographs.
*Wild Flowers.* John Hutchinson (Penguin).
*Wild Flowers of Europe.* Lorna F. Bowden (Hamlyn).
*Mountain Flowers.* A. Huxley (Blandford).
*Wild Flowers of Britain.* Roger Phillips (Pan). Very good photographs.

# Clubs to Join

*The Council for Environmental Conservation* (address: Zoological Gardens, Regent's Park, London NW1 4RY) will supply the addresses of your local *Natural History Societies.* (Send a stamped self-addressed envelope for a free list.) Many of these have wild flower sections and almost all have field meetings. *The Royal Society for Nature Conservation* (address: 22 The Green, Nettleham, Lincoln) will give you the address of your local *County Naturalist Trust*, which may have a junior branch. Many of the Trusts have meetings, lectures, and offer opportunities for work on reserves.
*London Natural History Society* The Secretary, 21 Green Way, Frinton on Sea, Essex, and the *Botanical Society of the British Isles,* c/o The Natural History Museum,

Cromwell Road, London SW7. Both societies encourage young members, but their journals are quite advanced and it would be best to join when you really know your wild flowers.
*The British Naturalist Association* (Mrs K. L. Butcher, Willowfield, Boynes Wood Road, Four Marks, Alton, Hants) would be more suitable for you to join.
One of the best societies to join is *The Wild Flower Society* (address: c/o Harvest House, 62 London Road, Reading ). They help you with identification, organize competitions, and when you join, give you a collecting diary where you can record every wild flower that you spot.

# Latin Names of Flowers

The English name of a flower may vary from one part of the country to another and this can often be very confusing. If you look up a flower in other books, you may find that it helps to know the flower's name in Latin as well. This list gives the Latin names of the flowers in this book, in the order in which they appear. The first name given for each page refers to the flower at the top of that page, and so on, reading down the page.

# Wild Flowers Scorecard

The flowers in this scorecard are arranged in alphabetical order. When you go spotting, fill in the date at the top of one of the blank columns, and then write in that column your score, next to each flower that you see. At the end of the day, add up your scores and put the total at the bottom of the columns. Then add up your grand total.

| Name of flower | Score | Date | Date | Date | Name of flower | Score | | | |
|---|---|---|---|---|---|---|---|---|---|
| Agrimony, Hemp | 10 | | | | Celandine, Lesser | 5 | | | |
| Anemone, Wood | 10 | | | | Centaury, Common | 10 | | | |
| Archangel, Yellow | 10 | | | | Chamomile, Wild | 15 | | | |
| Balsam, Touch-me-not | 25 | | | | Chickweed | 5 | | | |
| Barberry | 10 | | | | Chickweed, Field Mouse-ear | 15 | | | |
| Bats-in-the-Belfry | 15 | | | | Cinquefoil, Creeping | 5 | | | |
| Bilberry | 10 | | | | Clary, Meadow | 20 | | | |
| Bindweed, Greater | 10 | | | | Clover, White | 5 | | | |
| Bistort | 10 | | | | Cornflower | 25 | | | |
| Blackberry | 5 | | | | Cowslip | 10 | | | |
| Bluebell | 10 | | | | Creeping Jenny | 15 | | | |
| Brooklime | 10 | | | | Cress, Alpine Rock | 20 | | | |
| Bryony, White | 15 | | | | Daisy | 5 | | | |
| Bugle | 10 | | | | Daisy, Ox-eye | 10 | | | |
| Bugloss, Viper's | 10 | | | | Dandelion | 5 | | | |
| Buttercup, Creeping | 5 | | | | Dead-Nettle, White | 5 | | | |
| Campion, Bladder | 10 | | | | Dropwort, Corky-fruited | 25 | | | |
| Campion, Red | 10 | | | | Forget-me-not, Common | 10 | | | |
| Campion, White | 10 | | | | Foxglove | 10 | | | |
| Carrot, Wild | 10 | | | | Fritillary | 20 | | | |
| | | | | | | | | | |
| Total | | | | | Total | | | | |

| Name of flower | Score | | | | Name of flower | Score | | | |
|---|---|---|---|---|---|---|---|---|---|
| Frogbit | 15 | | | | Meadowsweet | 10 | | | |
| Fumitory, Common | 10 | | | | Mercury, Dog's | 10 | | | |
| Furze | 10 | | | | Monkshood, Common | 20 | | | |
| Garlic, Triangular-Stalked | 20 | | | | Nettle | 5 | | | |
| Geranium, Blood-red | 10 | | | | Nightshade, Black | 10 | | | |
| Golden Rod | 10 | | | | Orache, Common | 5 | | | |
| Good King Henry | 5 | | | | Orchid, Early Purple | 15 | | | |
| Goosegrass | 5 | | | | Pansy, Wild | 10 | | | |
| Groundsel, Wood | 15 | | | | Parsley, Cow | 5 | | | |
| Heather (or Ling) | 5 | | | | Parsley, Hedge | 15 | | | |
| Heather, Bell | 15 | | | | Pasque Flower | 25 | | | |
| Helleborine, Red | 25 | | | | Pea, Wild | 20 | | | |
| Herb Bennet | 10 | | | | Pellitory-of-the-Wall | 15 | | | |
| Herb Robert | 10 | | | | Periwinkle, Lesser | 15 | | | |
| Hogweed | 5 | | | | Pheasant's Eye | 25 | | | |
| Holly, Sea | 15 | | | | Pheasant's Eye, Summer | 25 | | | |
| Houseleek | 15 | | | | Pigweed | 10 | | | |
| Jack-by-the-Hedge | 5 | | | | Pimpernel, Scarlet | 10 | | | |
| Knapweed | 10 | | | | Pimpernel, Yellow | 10 | | | |
| Knotgrass | 5 | | | | Pink, Deptford | 25 | | | |
| Larkspur | 15 | | | | Plantain, Floating Water | 15 | | | |
| Lily-of-the-Valley | 15 | | | | Plantain, Greater | 5 | | | |
| Meadow Rue Common | 15 | | | | Plantain, Hoary | 5 | | | |
| Total | | | | | Total | | | | |

| Name of flower | Score | | | | Name of flower | Score | | | |
|---|---|---|---|---|---|---|---|---|---|
| Plantain, Ribwort | 5 | | | | Sorrel | 5 | | | |
| Policeman's Helmet | 15 | | | | Sorrel, Sheep's | 15 | | | |
| Poppy | 10 | | | | Sorrel, Wood | 5 | | | |
| Poppy, Long-headed | 5 | | | | Speedwell, Common | 10 | | | |
| Primrose | 10 | | | | Spurge, Cypress | 15 | | | |
| Purslane | 15 | | | | Spurrey, Corn | 10 | | | |
| Ragged Robin | 15 | | | | Spurrey, Sand | 10 | | | |
| Ramsons | 15 | | | | Stitchwort, Greater | 5 | | | |
| Rape | 5 | | | | Stonecrop | 10 | | | |
| Rose, Dog | 15 | | | | Strawberry, Wild | 15 | | | |
| St John's Wort, Common | 10 | | | | Sweet William | 20 | | | |
| Saxifrage, Alternate-Leaved Golden | 15 | | | | Toadflax, Ivy-leaved | 5 | | | |
| Saxifrage, Meadow | 20 | | | | Trefoil, Bird's Foot | 10 | | | |
| Saxifrage, Starry | 15 | | | | Vetch, Tufted | 10 | | | |
| Scabious, Devil's Bit | 10 | | | | Violet, Common Dog | 10 | | | |
| Scabious, Field | 10 | | | | Water Crowfoot | 10 | | | |
| Shepherd's Purse | 5 | | | | Water Soldier | 25 | | | |
| Silverweed | 10 | | | | Willowherb, Rosebay | 5 | | | |
| Snapdragon | 5 | | | | Woad | 20 | | | |
| Snowdrop | 15 | | | | Woundwort, Wood | 10 | | | |
| Soapwort | 20 | | | | Yarrow | 5 | | | |
| | | | | | | | | | |
| Total | | | | | Total | | | | |

Grand Total

# Part 2
# TREES

# Introduction to Part 2

This section of the book will help you to identify over 80 different trees, and also some shrubs. Take the book when you go out spotting. Not all of the trees shown will be common in your area, but look in large parks and gardens, and you will be able to track down many of them.

There is a list of places to visit on page 124. These places have some of the more unusual species of trees, as well as more common ones.

When using the book, remember that the shape of trees can vary a great deal. The Noble Fir that you spot, for example, may not have the same sort of crown as the one shown on page 78. This is because young trees often look very different from middle-aged or mature trees of the same species. In this section, we have tried to show only mature trees (that is, those that are fully grown).

**Acknowledgements**
The illustrators would like to acknowledge help of the staff of the Royal Botanical Gardens at Kew, with special thanks to Ruth Messor. They also thank Dr Martin Rix at the Royal Horticultural Society Gardens at Wisley, and Peter Orriss of the Cambridge University Botanical Gardens.

# Identifying Trees with this Book

This section is arranged with conifers first, followed by broad-leaved trees and shrubs. Trees that are closely related, for example all the Oaks, are grouped together.

The illustrations show important features that will help you to identify a tree at any time of the year. For each type of tree, the leaf, the bark, the shape of a full-grown tree in full leaf and its shape in winter (if the tree is deciduous) are always shown. Flowers and fruits (including cones) are also illustrated if they will help you to identify the tree.

The description next to each illustration gives you additional information to help you identify trees. The average height of a full-grown tree is written next to each illustration.

Remember that there are many clues to help you recognize a tree, not just the leaves, so look carefully at the bark, the tree's shape and other features.

If the tree you want to identify has no leaves on it in winter, you may be able to find out what it is by examining its winter buds and the shape of its twigs. Some of these are shown on pages 116-7. Look for others in the books listed on page 124.

Flower

Leaf   Fruits

Height of tree in metres

Bark

Tree in winter

Beside the description is a small blank circle. Each time you spot a new tree, make a tick in the circle.

## Scorecard

On pages 127-8 there is a score-card which gives you a score for each tree you spot. A common tree scores 5 points, and a very rare one is worth 25 points. If you like, you can add up your score after a day out spotting.

| Name of tree | Score | Date Mar 2 | Date Mar 10 | Date Apr 3 |
|---|---|---|---|---|
| Acacia, False | 10 | 10 | 10 | 10 |
| Alder, Common | 5 | | 5 | |
| Alder, Grey | 15 | | | |

# Parts of a Tree

A tree is a plant that grows on a single, central woody stem. A shrub is usually smaller and has many stems.

Trees are divided into two main groups: **conifers** and **broadleaved trees.** Most broadleaved trees have broad flat leaves (which they drop in winter) and they have seeds which are enclosed in fruits (nuts or other forms). Most conifers have narrow, needle-like or scaly leaves. Their fruits are usually woody cones.

Most broadleaved trees are **deciduous** which means that they lose their leaves in the autumn and grow new ones again in the spring. Most conifers are **evergreen,** meaning that they keep their green leaves throughout the winter.

These pictures show the different parts of a tree and explain some of the words that appear in the book.

## Leaves

There are many different shapes of leaves. Some of the most common ones are shown here.

A leaf that is in one piece is called **simple.**

A leaf that is made up of many **leaflets** is called **compound.**

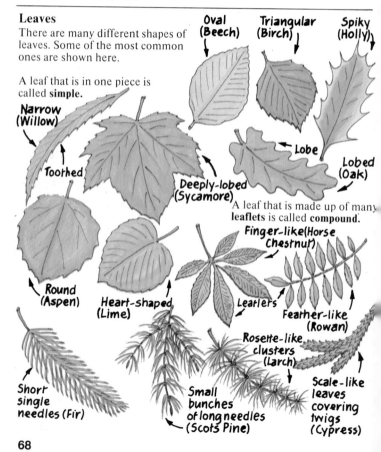

Oval (Beech)

Triangular (Birch)

Spiky (Holly)

Narrow (Willow)

Toothed

Lobe

Lobed (Oak)

Deeply-lobed (Sycamore)

Finger-like (Horse Chestnut)

Leaflets

Feather-like (Rowan)

Round (Aspen)

Heart-shaped (Lime)

Rosette-like clusters (Larch)

Scale-like leaves covering twigs (Cypress)

Short single needles (Fir)

Small bunches of long needles (Scots Pine)

# Flowers

All trees have flowers that develop into fruits. Here are some different types of flowers.

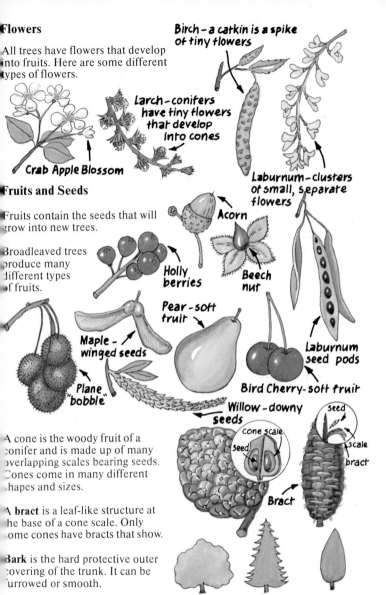

Birch – a catkin is a spike of tiny flowers

Larch – conifers have tiny flowers that develop into cones

Crab Apple Blossom

Laburnum – clusters of small, separate flowers

# Fruits and Seeds

Fruits contain the seeds that will grow into new trees.

Broadleaved trees produce many different types of fruits.

Acorn

Holly berries

Beech nut

Pear – soft fruit

Maple – winged seeds

Plane "bobble"

Laburnum seed pods

Bird Cherry – soft fruit

Willow – downy seeds

cone scale

seed

seed

scale

bract

Bract

A cone is the woody fruit of a conifer and is made up of many overlapping scales bearing seeds. Cones come in many different shapes and sizes.

A **bract** is a leaf-like structure at the base of a cone scale. Only some cones have bracts that show.

**Bark** is the hard protective outer covering of the trunk. It can be furrowed or smooth.

The **crown** of a tree is its leafy top. Crown shapes vary a lot.

Broad (Oak)

Cone-shaped (Norway Spruce)

Narrow (Lombardy Poplar)

# Conifers

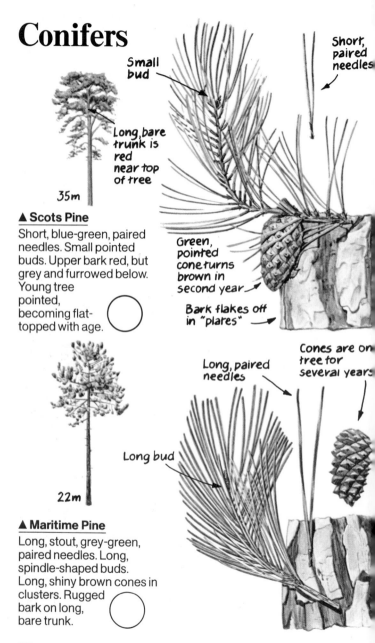

Small bud

Short, paired needles

Long, bare trunk is red near top of tree

35m

## ▲ Scots Pine

Short, blue-green, paired needles. Small pointed buds. Upper bark red, but grey and furrowed below. Young tree pointed, becoming flat-topped with age.

Green, pointed cone turns brown in second year

Bark flakes off in "plates"

Cones are on tree for several years

Long, paired needles

Long bud

22m

## ▲ Maritime Pine

Long, stout, grey-green, paired needles. Long, spindle-shaped buds. Long, shiny brown cones in clusters. Rugged bark on long, bare trunk.

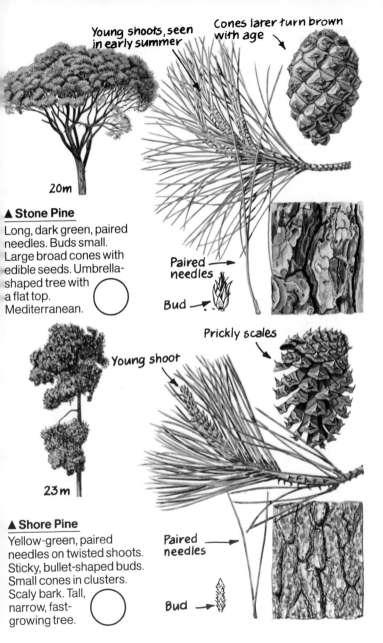

Young shoots, seen in early summer

Cones later turn brown with age

## ▲ Stone Pine

Long, dark green, paired needles. Buds small. Large broad cones with edible seeds. Umbrella-shaped tree with a flat top. Mediterranean.

20m

Paired needles

Bud

Prickly scales

Young shoot

## ▲ Shore Pine

Yellow-green, paired needles on twisted shoots. Sticky, bullet-shaped buds. Small cones in clusters. Scaly bark. Tall, narrow, fast-growing tree.

23 m

Paired needles

Bud

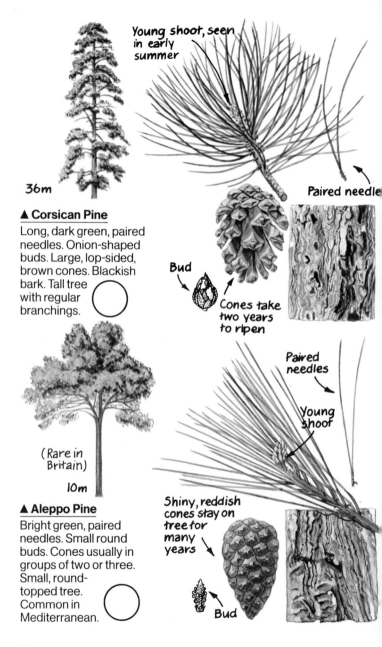

Young shoot, seen in early summer

Paired needle

36m

## ▲ Corsican Pine

Long, dark green, paired needles. Onion-shaped buds. Large, lop-sided, brown cones. Blackish bark. Tall tree with regular branchings.

Bud

Cones take two years to ripen

Paired needles

Young shoot

(Rare in Britain)

10m

## ▲ Aleppo Pine

Bright green, paired needles. Small round buds. Cones usually in groups of two or three. Small, round-topped tree. Common in Mediterranean.

Shiny, reddish cones stay on tree for many years

Bud

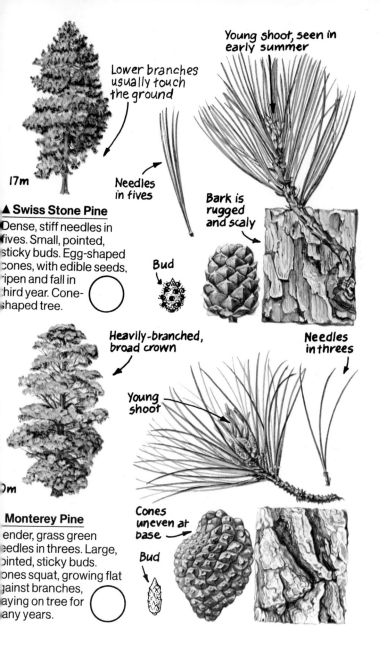

Young shoot, seen in early summer

Lower branches usually touch the ground

17m

Needles in fives

Bark is rugged and scaly

Bud

### ▲ Swiss Stone Pine

Dense, stiff needles in fives. Small, pointed, sticky buds. Egg-shaped cones, with edible seeds, ripen and fall in third year. Cone-shaped tree.

Heavily-branched, broad crown

Needles in threes

Young shoot

0m

Cones uneven at base

Bud

### Monterey Pine

Slender, grass green needles in threes. Large, pointed, sticky buds. Cones squat, growing flat against branches, staying on tree for many years.

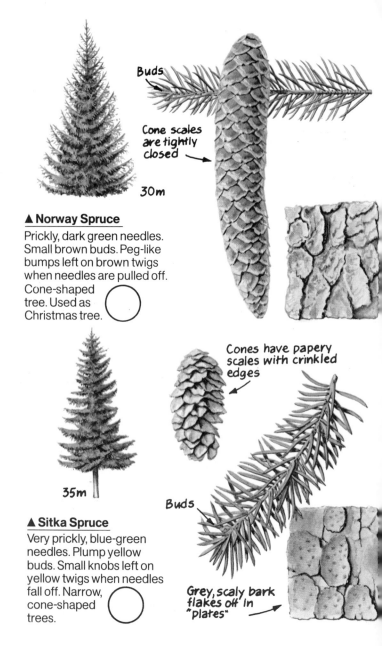

Buds

Cone scales are tightly closed

30m

## ▲ Norway Spruce

Prickly, dark green needles. Small brown buds. Peg-like bumps left on brown twigs when needles are pulled off. Cone-shaped tree. Used as Christmas tree.

Cones have papery scales with crinkled edges

35m

## ▲ Sitka Spruce

Very prickly, blue-green needles. Plump yellow buds. Small knobs left on yellow twigs when needles fall off. Narrow, cone-shaped trees.

Buds

Grey, scaly bark flakes off in "plates"

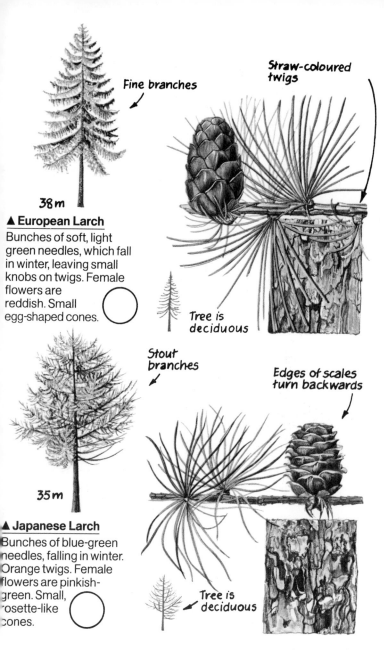

Fine branches

Straw-coloured twigs

**38 m**

## ▲ European Larch

Bunches of soft, light green needles, which fall in winter, leaving small knobs on twigs. Female flowers are reddish. Small egg-shaped cones.

Tree is deciduous

Stout branches

Edges of scales turn backwards

**35 m**

## ▲ Japanese Larch

Bunches of blue-green needles, falling in winter. Orange twigs. Female flowers are pinkish-green. Small, rosette-like cones.

Tree is deciduous

75

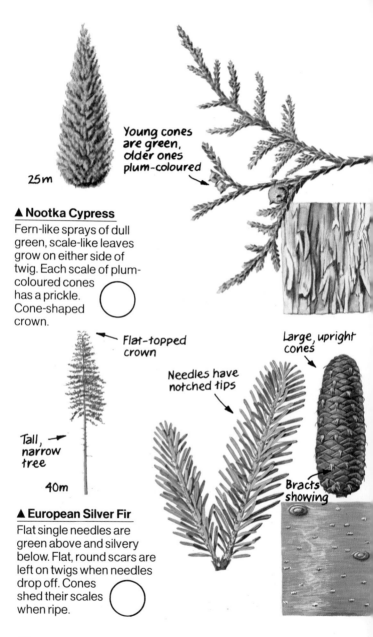

**Young cones are green, older ones plum-coloured**

25m

### ▲ Nootka Cypress

Fern-like sprays of dull green, scale-like leaves grow on either side of twig. Each scale of plum-coloured cones has a prickle. Cone-shaped crown.

Flat-topped crown

Large, upright cones

Needles have notched tips

Tall, narrow tree

40m

Bracts showing

### ▲ European Silver Fir

Flat single needles are green above and silvery below. Flat, round scars are left on twigs when needles drop off. Cones shed their scales when ripe.

30m

## ▲ Greek Fir

Shiny green, spiny-tipped
needles all round twig.
Tall, narrow cones shed
scales to leave bare
spike on
tree. Common
in parks.

Pointed tip

Bark flakes off
in "plates"

28m

## Spanish Fir

Short, blunt, blue-grey
needles all round twig.
Cylindrical, upright cones
fall apart on tree.
Found only in
gardens in Britain.

Blunt tip

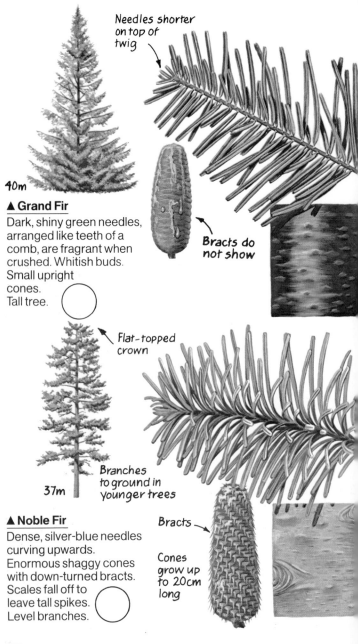

Needles shorter on top of twig

**40m**

### ▲ Grand Fir

Dark, shiny green needles, arranged like teeth of a comb, are fragrant when crushed. Whitish buds. Small upright cones. Tall tree.

Bracts do not show

Flat-topped crown

Branches to ground in younger trees

**37m**

### ▲ Noble Fir

Dense, silver-blue needles curving upwards. Enormous shaggy cones with down-turned bracts. Scales fall off to leave tall spikes. Level branches.

Bracts

Cones grow up to 20cm long

Beech-like bud

Needles are parted on twig

Bracts

## ▲ Douglas Fir

Soft fragrant needles.
Long-pointed, copper-
brown buds. Light brown,
hanging cones with three-
pointed bracts.
Old bark is thick
and corky.

Leader droops

Young cones are green, older ones are brown

Cone has a few rounded scales

Tips of branches droop

35m

## Western Hemlock

Needles various lengths,
green above and silver
below. Small cones on
shoot tips. Smooth, brown
scaly bark.
Branch tips and
top shoot droops.

Flattened needles

40m

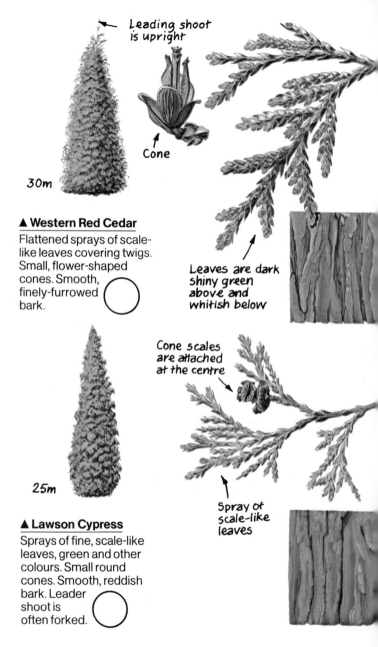

Leading shoot is upright

Cone

**▲ Western Red Cedar**

Flattened sprays of scale-like leaves covering twigs. Small, flower-shaped cones. Smooth, finely-furrowed bark.

30m

Leaves are dark shiny green above and whitish below

Cone scales are attached at the centre

Spray of scale-like leaves

**▲ Lawson Cypress**

Sprays of fine, scale-like leaves, green and other colours. Small round cones. Smooth, reddish bark. Leader shoot is often forked.

25m

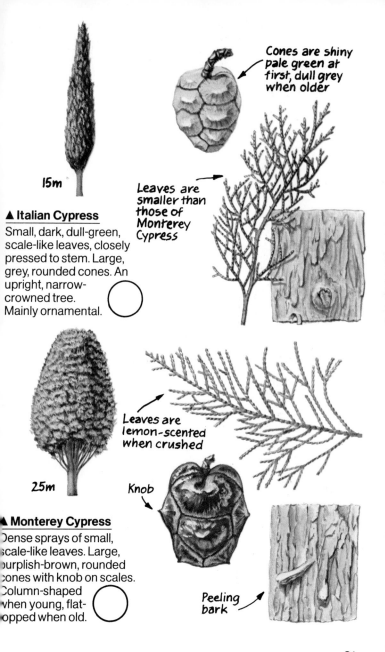

Cones are shiny pale green at first, dull grey when older

**15m**

Leaves are smaller than those of Monterey Cypress

### ▲ Italian Cypress

Small, dark, dull-green, scale-like leaves, closely pressed to stem. Large, grey, rounded cones. An upright, narrow-crowned tree. Mainly ornamental.

Leaves are lemon-scented when crushed

**25m**

Knob

### ▲ Monterey Cypress

Dense sprays of small, scale-like leaves. Large, purplish-brown, rounded cones with knob on scales. Column-shaped when young, flat-topped when old.

Peeling bark

81

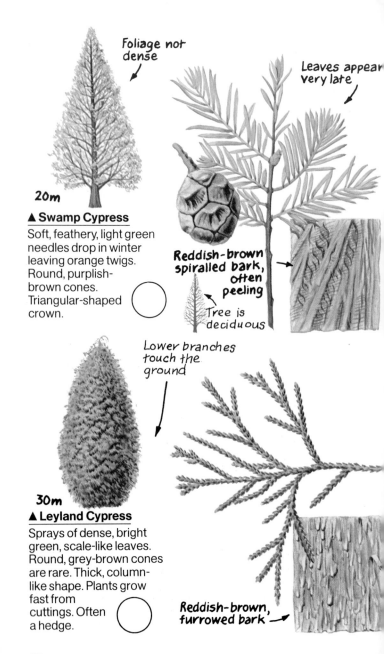

Foliage not dense

Leaves appear very late

**20m**

**▲ Swamp Cypress**
Soft, feathery, light green needles drop in winter leaving orange twigs. Round, purplish-brown cones. Triangular-shaped crown.

Reddish-brown spiralled bark, often peeling

Tree is deciduous

Lower branches touch the ground

**30m**

**▲ Leyland Cypress**
Sprays of dense, bright green, scale-like leaves. Round, grey-brown cones are rare. Thick, column-like shape. Plants grow fast from cuttings. Often a hedge.

Reddish-brown, furrowed bark

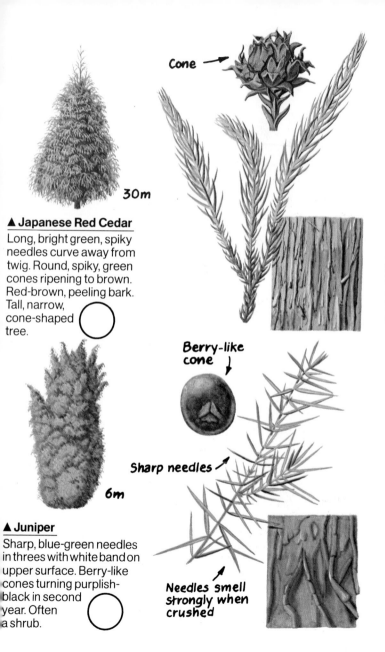

Cone

**30m**

## ▲ Japanese Red Cedar
Long, bright green, spiky needles curve away from twig. Round, spiky, green cones ripening to brown. Red-brown, peeling bark. Tall, narrow, cone-shaped tree.

**6m**

## ▲ Juniper
Sharp, blue-green needles in threes with white band on upper surface. Berry-like cones turning purplish-black in second year. Often a shrub.

Berry-like cone

Sharp needles

Needles smell strongly when crushed

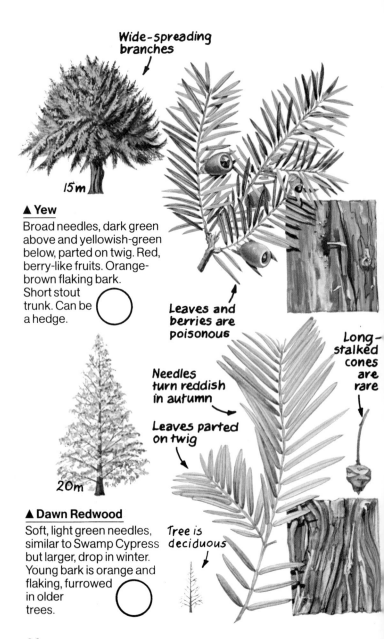

Wide-spreading branches

15m

### ▲ Yew

Broad needles, dark green above and yellowish-green below, parted on twig. Red, berry-like fruits. Orange-brown flaking bark. Short stout trunk. Can be a hedge.

Leaves and berries are poisonous

Long-stalked cones are rare

Needles turn reddish in autumn

Leaves parted on twig

20m

### ▲ Dawn Redwood

Soft, light green needles, similar to Swamp Cypress but larger, drop in winter. Young bark is orange and flaking, furrowed in older trees.

Tree is deciduous

**33m**

### ▲ Coast Redwood

Hard, sharp-pointed needles, dark green above and white-banded below. Small, round cones. Thick, reddish, spongy bark. Tall tree.

Needles parted on either side of twig →

Foliage hanging from upswept branches ↙

**38m**

### ▲ Wellingtonia

Deep green, scale-like, pointed leaves. Long-stalked, round, corky cones. Soft, thick, deeply-furrowed bark. Tall tree with upswept branches.

Diamond-shaped cone scales wrinkle when they ripen ↓

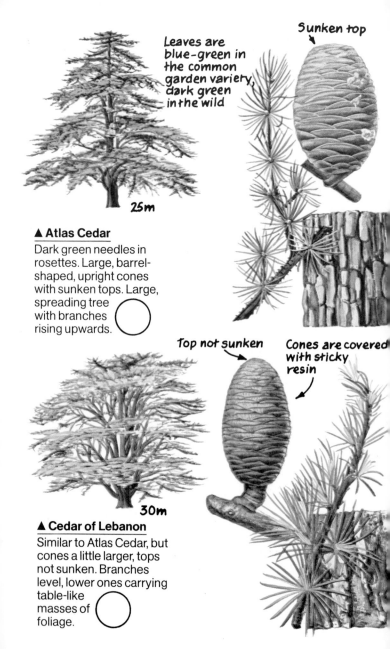

Leaves are blue-green in the common garden variety, dark green in the wild

Sunken top

## ▲ Atlas Cedar

Dark green needles in rosettes. Large, barrel-shaped, upright cones with sunken tops. Large, spreading tree with branches rising upwards.

25m

Top not sunken

Cones are covered with sticky resin

## ▲ Cedar of Lebanon

Similar to Atlas Cedar, but cones a little larger, tops not sunken. Branches level, lower ones carrying table-like masses of foliage.

30m

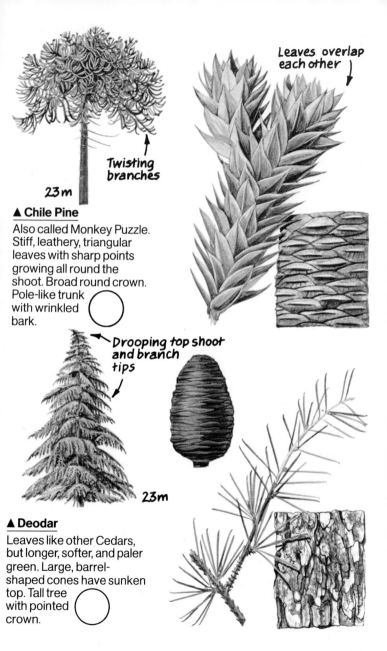

Leaves overlap each other ↓

Twisting branches

23 m

## ▲ Chile Pine

Also called Monkey Puzzle. Stiff, leathery, triangular leaves with sharp points growing all round the shoot. Broad round crown. Pole-like trunk with wrinkled bark.

Drooping top shoot and branch tips

23 m

## ▲ Deodar

Leaves like other Cedars, but longer, softer, and paler green. Large, barrel-shaped cones have sunken top. Tall tree with pointed crown.

# Broadleaved Trees

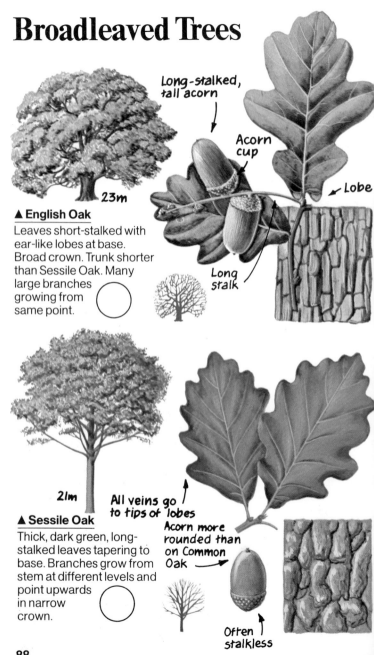

Long-stalked, tall acorn

Acorn cup

Lobe

**23m**

**▲ English Oak**
Leaves short-stalked with
ear-like lobes at base.
Broad crown. Trunk shorter
than Sessile Oak. Many
large branches
growing from
same point.

Long
stalk

**21m**

All veins go
to tips of lobes

**▲ Sessile Oak**
Thick, dark green, long-
stalked leaves tapering to
base. Branches grow from
stem at different levels and
point upwards
in narrow
crown.

Acorn more
rounded than
on Common
Oak

Often
stalkless

Leaf shape varies

Teeth

← Evergreen leaves

Small acorn, almost covered by cup

## ▲ Holm Oak

Shiny evergreen leaves, greyish-green beneath, sometimes with shallow teeth like Holly leaves. Common ornamental tree. Broad dense crown.

20m

## Turkey Oak

Leaves unevenly lobed and saw-toothed. Whiskers on buds and at base of leaves. Acorn cups mossy and stalkless. Acorns ripen second autumn.

25m

Acorn cup is mossy

89

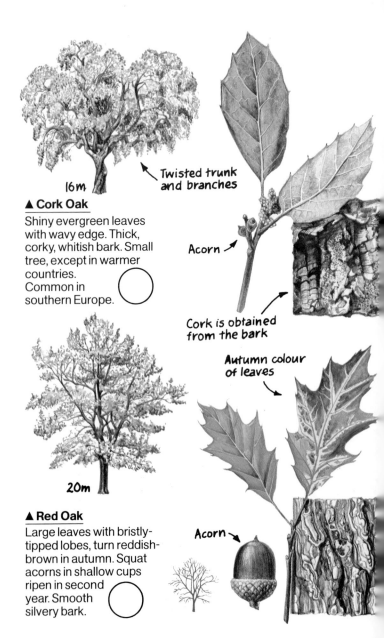

**16m**

▲ **Cork Oak**

Shiny evergreen leaves with wavy edge. Thick, corky, whitish bark. Small tree, except in warmer countries.
Common in southern Europe.

Twisted trunk and branches

Acorn →

Cork is obtained from the bark

Autumn colour of leaves

**20m**

▲ **Red Oak**

Large leaves with bristly-tipped lobes, turn reddish-brown in autumn. Squat acorns in shallow cups ripen in second year. Smooth silvery bark.

Acorn →

25m

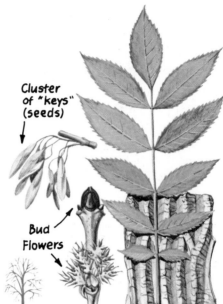

Cluster of "keys" (seeds)

Bud

Flowers

### ▲ Common Ash
Compound leaf of 9-13 leaflets appearing late, after bunches of purplish flowers. Clusters of "keys" stay on the tree into winter. Pale grey bark.

20m

Fruit

Flowers

Leaflets downy near veins

### ▲ Manna Ash
Compound leaf of 5-9 stalked leaflets. Clusters of showy white flowers in May. Smooth grey bark oozes sugary liquid called manna.

Leaf has notched tip

Cone-like fruit stays on all winter

**12m**

## ▲ Common Alder

Leaves rounded, falling in late autumn. Young twigs and leaves sticky. Reddish catkins. Fruits like small, brown, woody cones. Always near water.

Green fruits ripen into brown, woody "cones" (shown above)

**14m**

## ▲ Grey Alder

Pointed oval leaves with sharply-toothed edge, soft and grey underneath. Twigs and bark grey. Catkins and fruit like Common Alder.

**Berries**

One flower
(from a
cluster)

Toothed
edge

Leaves
turn red
in Autumn

## Rowan

ompound leaf like Ash,
t smaller. Clusters of
eamy-white flowers in
ay. Red berries ripen in
ugust. Small tree.
ten grows alone
mountainsides.

**7m**

## Whitebeam

rge oval leaves with
othed edge, white and
ry underneath. Flowers
d fruit like Rowan but
en later.
ows at edges
woods.

**8m**

**Berries**

Leaf stalk is flattened →

**20m**

## ▲ Aspen

Rounded leaves with wavy edge, trembling in wind. White downy catkins. Grey bark with large pores. Smaller than other Poplars. Often in thickets.

Fan-shaped crown

**25m**

## ▲ Black Italian Poplar

Dark green, triangular, pointed leaves, appearing late. Red catkins. Deeply furrowed bark. Trunk and crown often lean away from wind. Grows fast.

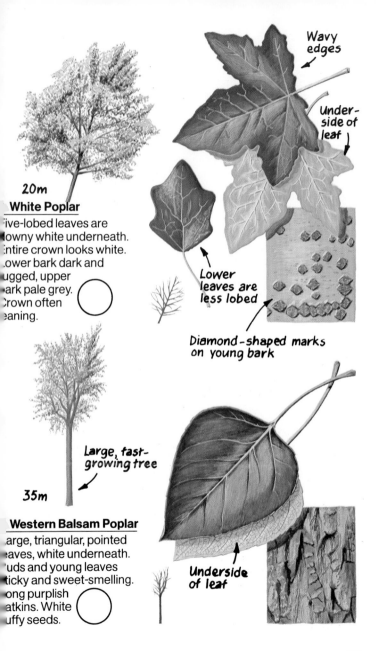

Wavy edges

Under-side of leaf

**20m**

## White Poplar

Five-lobed leaves are downy white underneath. Entire crown looks white. Lower bark dark and rugged, upper bark pale grey. Crown often leaning.

Lower leaves are less lobed

Diamond-shaped marks on young bark

Large, fast-growing tree

**35m**

## Western Balsam Poplar

Large, triangular, pointed leaves, white underneath. Buds and young leaves sticky and sweet-smelling. Long purplish catkins. White fluffy seeds.

Underside of leaf

Leaf shape varies

28m

### ▲ Lombardy Poplar

Pointed triangular leaves.
Tall narrow tree. Branches
grow upwards from
ground. Furrowed
bark. Often along
roadsides.

High-domed crown

Leaf from upper branch

Rounded leaf from lower branch

23m

### ▲ Grey Poplar

Similar to White Poplar.
Wavy-edged leaves, never
deeply lobed, downy white
underneath. Upper bark
yellowish-grey,
lower bark
dark, furrowed.

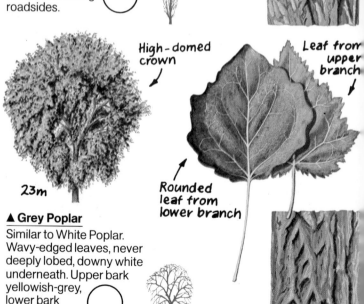

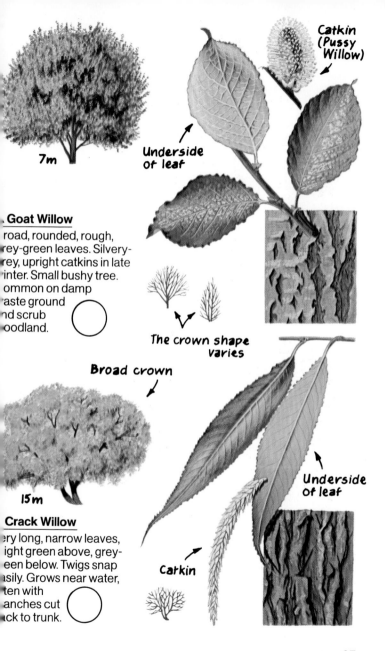

Catkin
(Pussy
Willow)

Underside
of leaf

**Goat Willow**

road, rounded, rough,
rey-green leaves. Silvery-
rey, upright catkins in late
inter. Small bushy tree.
ommon on damp
aste ground
nd scrub
oodland.

7m

The crown shape
varies

Broad crown

15m

**Crack Willow**

ery long, narrow leaves,
ight green above, grey-
een below. Twigs snap
sily. Grows near water,
ten with
anches cut
ck to trunk.

Underside
of leaf

Catkin

97

**20m**

**▲ White Willow**

Long, narrow, finely-toothed leaves, white underneath. Slender twigs, hard to break. Common by water. Weeping Willow is a variety with trailing branches.

Underside of leaf →

Catkin ↓

**15m**

**▲ Silver Birch**

Small, diamond-shaped leaves with double-toothed edge. Long "lamb's tail" catkins in April. Slender tree with drooping branches.

Catkin

Silvery bark peels off in ribbons →

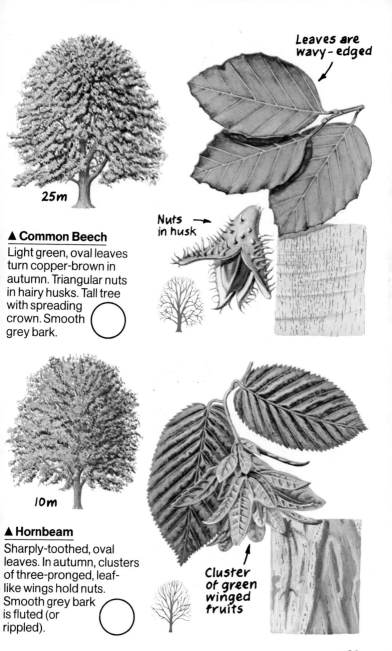

**Leaves are wavy-edged**

25m

**Nuts in husk**

## ▲ Common Beech
Light green, oval leaves turn copper-brown in autumn. Triangular nuts in hairy husks. Tall tree with spreading crown. Smooth grey bark.

10m

## ▲ Hornbeam
Sharply-toothed, oval leaves. In autumn, clusters of three-pronged, leaf-like wings hold nuts. Smooth grey bark is fluted (or rippled).

**Cluster of green winged fruits**

99

**▲ Crab Apple**

Small rounded leaves with toothed edge. Pinkish-white flowers in May. Small, speckled, reddish-green apples. Small bushy tree. Common in hedges.

10 m

Apple tastes sour

**▲ Common Pear**

Small, dark green, oval leaves with long stalks. Large, showy, white flowers in April. Small pears are gritty to eat. Tall narrow tree. In woods and hedgerows.

15 m

Pear is golden when ripe

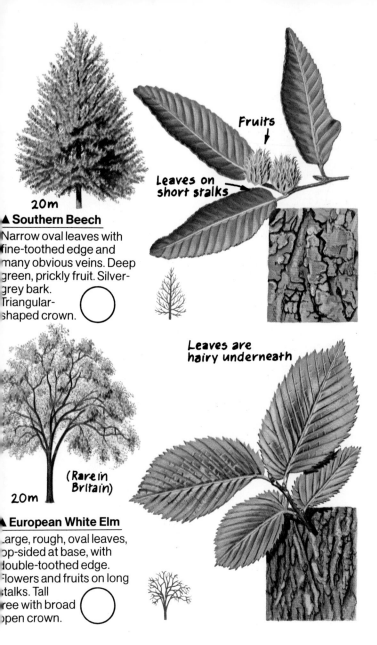

**20m**

## ▲ Southern Beech

Narrow oval leaves with fine-toothed edge and many obvious veins. Deep green, prickly fruit. Silver-grey bark. Triangular-shaped crown.

Fruits

Leaves on short stalks

Leaves are hairy underneath

(Rare in Britain)

**20m**

## ▲ European White Elm

Large, rough, oval leaves, lop-sided at base, with double-toothed edge. Flowers and fruits on long stalks. Tall tree with broad open crown.

**30m**

### ▲ London Plane

Large broad leaves with pointed lobes. Spiny "bobble" fruits hanging all winter. Flaking bark leaving yellowish patches. Tall tree, often in towns.

*Fruit*

**20m**

### ▲ Sycamore

Dark green, leathery leaves with five lobes. Paired, closely-angled, winged seeds. Large spreading tree. Smooth brown bark becoming scaly.

*Toothed edge*

*Seeds twist as they fall*

Leaves turn golden in autumn

15m

## ▲ Norway Maple

Light green, thin leaves. Lobes and teeth are bristle-tipped. Paired seeds form wide angle. Smaller, less spreading than Sycamore. Finely-furrowed, grey bark.

Pairs of seeds spin as they fall

Lobes are blunt

Leaves turn golden in autumn

10m

## ▲ Field Maple

Small, dark green leaves with five lobes. Small, reddish, winged seeds form a straight line. Small tree with round head. Often in hedges.

Seeds

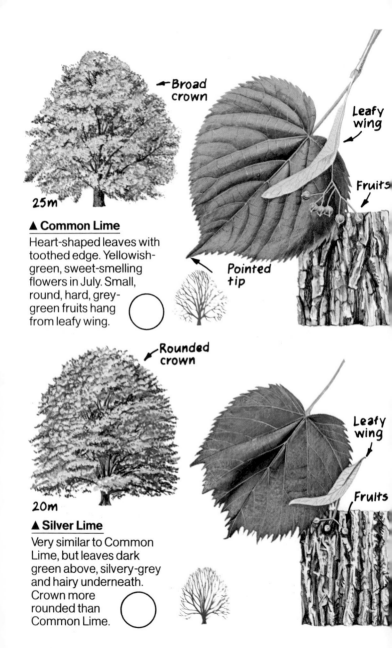

**Broad crown**

25m

**Leafy wing**

**Fruits**

### ▲ Common Lime

Heart-shaped leaves with toothed edge. Yellowish-green, sweet-smelling flowers in July. Small, round, hard, grey-green fruits hang from leafy wing.

**Pointed tip**

**Rounded crown**

20m

**Leafy wing**

**Fruits**

### ▲ Silver Lime

Very similar to Common Lime, but leaves dark green above, silvery-grey and hairy underneath. Crown more rounded than Common Lime.

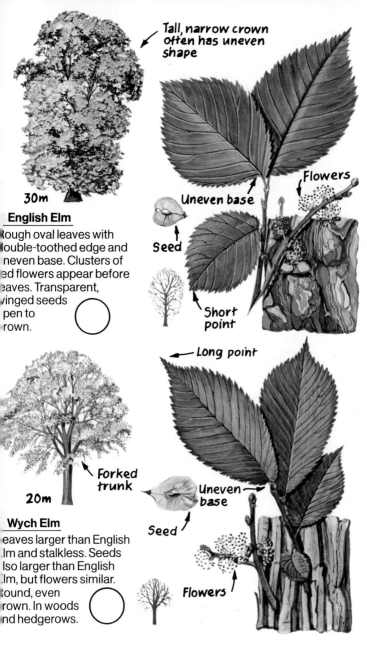

Tall, narrow crown often has uneven shape

**English Elm**

Rough oval leaves with double-toothed edge and uneven base. Clusters of red flowers appear before leaves. Transparent, winged seeds open to crown.

30m

Flowers

Uneven base

Seed

Short point

Long point

**Wych Elm**

Leaves larger than English Elm and stalkless. Seeds also larger than English Elm, but flowers similar. Round, even crown. In woods and hedgerows.

20m

Forked trunk

Uneven base

Seed

Flowers

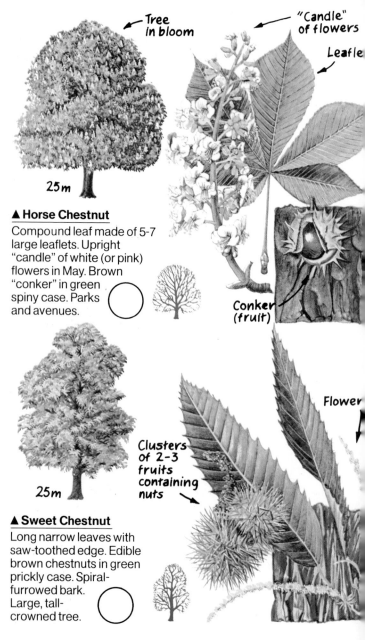

Tree
in bloom

"Candle"
of flowers

Leafle

25 m

## ▲ Horse Chestnut

Compound leaf made of 5-7
large leaflets. Upright
"candle" of white (or pink)
flowers in May. Brown
"conker" in green
spiny case. Parks
and avenues.

Conker
(fruit)

25 m

## ▲ Sweet Chestnut

Long narrow leaves with
saw-toothed edge. Edible
brown chestnuts in green
prickly case. Spiral-
furrowed bark.
Large, tall-
crowned tree.

Flower

Clusters
of 2-3
fruits
containing
nuts

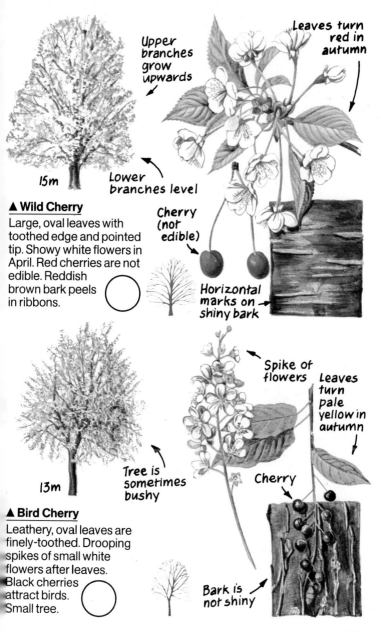

Upper
branches
grow
upwards

Lower
branches level

Leaves turn
red in
autumn

15m

### ▲ Wild Cherry
Large, oval leaves with
toothed edge and pointed
tip. Showy white flowers in
April. Red cherries are not
edible. Reddish
brown bark peels
in ribbons.

Cherry
(not
edible)

Horizontal
marks on
shiny bark

Spike of
flowers

Leaves
turn
pale
yellow in
autumn

Tree is
sometimes
bushy

13m

Cherry

### ▲ Bird Cherry
Leathery, oval leaves are
finely-toothed. Drooping
spikes of small white
flowers after leaves.
Black cherries
attract birds.
Small tree.

Bark is
not shiny

107

Unripe fruit

Ripe fruit

Young fruit

## ▲ Black Mulberry

Rough, heart-shaped leaves with toothed edge. Short catkins. Edible, blackish-red berries. Low, broad-crowned tree. Short trunk and twisted branches.

Old trees have branches to the ground and often lean over

Smooth, green case containing edible walnut

Young fruit

## ▲ Common Walnut

Compound leaves of 7-9 untoothed leaflets. Twigs are hollow, with cross-sections inside. Smooth grey bark with some cracks, or fissures. Broad crown.

Leaves are bronze when they first open, turning green later

12m

15m

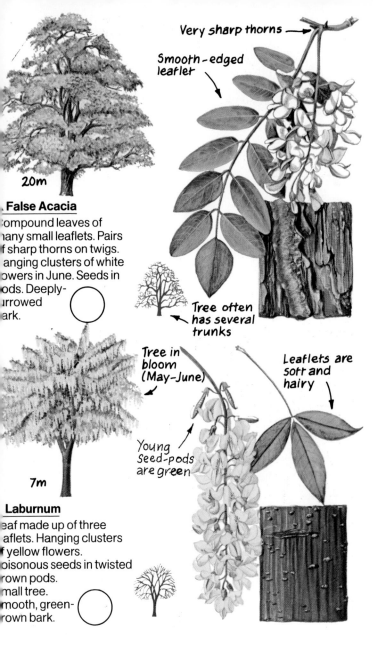

Very sharp thorns

Smooth-edged leaflet

20m

## False Acacia

Compound leaves of many small leaflets. Pairs of sharp thorns on twigs. Hanging clusters of white flowers in June. Seeds in pods. Deeply-furrowed bark.

Tree often has several trunks

Tree in bloom (May–June)

Leaflets are soft and hairy

Young seed-pods are green

7m

## Laburnum

Leaf made up of three leaflets. Hanging clusters of yellow flowers. Poisonous seeds in twisted brown pods. Small tree. Smooth, green-brown bark.

Leaves are thick
and leathery

Berries
appear only
on the female
trees

## ▲ Holly

Shiny, dark, evergreen
leaves with thorny prickles.
Small white flowers. Round
red berries. Smooth, grey-
green bark.
Small tree
or shrub.

Two kinds
of flower

10m

Flowers

## ▲ Tamarisk   Tree in bloom

3m

Tiny, grey-green, scale-
like leaves, which look
feathery. Clusters of small
pinkish-white flowers.
Shrub or small tree with
slender
branches. Often
near the sea.

Leaves

Twig

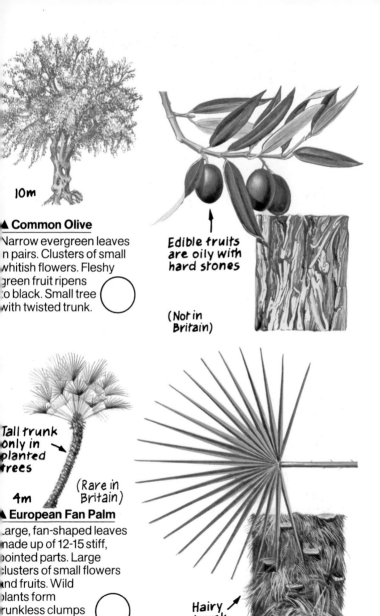

**10m**

## ▲ Common Olive

Narrow evergreen leaves in pairs. Clusters of small whitish flowers. Fleshy green fruit ripens to black. Small tree with twisted trunk.

Edible fruits are oily with hard stones

(Not in Britain)

Tall trunk only in planted trees

**4m**

(Rare in Britain)

## ▲ European Fan Palm

Large, fan-shaped leaves made up of 12-15 stiff, pointed parts. Large clusters of small flowers and fruits. Wild plants form trunkless clumps of leaves.

Hairy trunk

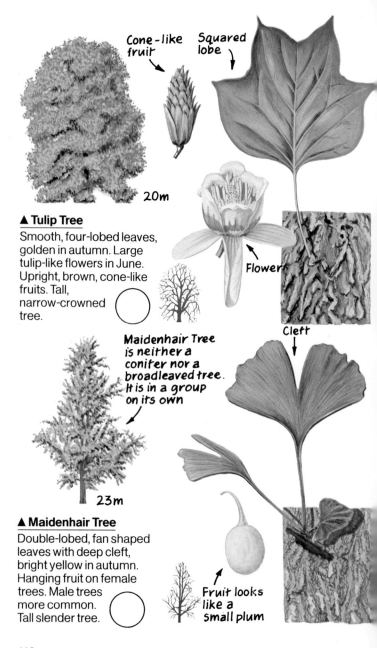

Cone-like fruit

Squared lobe

20m

### ▲ Tulip Tree

Smooth, four-lobed leaves, golden in autumn. Large tulip-like flowers in June. Upright, brown, cone-like fruits. Tall, narrow-crowned tree.

Flower

Cleft

Maidenhair Tree is neither a conifer nor a broadleaved tree. It is in a group on its own

23m

### ▲ Maidenhair Tree

Double-lobed, fan shaped leaves with deep cleft, bright yellow in autumn. Hanging fruit on female trees. Male trees more common. Tall slender tree.

Fruit looks like a small plum

# Shrubs

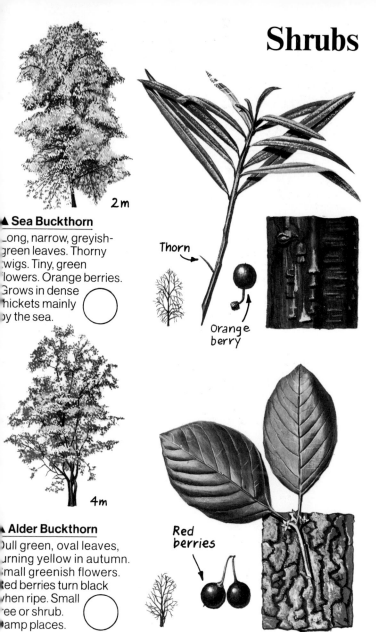

## ▲ Sea Buckthorn

Long, narrow, greyish-
green leaves. Thorny
twigs. Tiny, green
flowers. Orange berries.
Grows in dense
thickets mainly
by the sea.

2m

Thorn

Orange
berry

## ▲ Alder Buckthorn

Dull green, oval leaves,
turning yellow in autumn.
Small greenish flowers.
Red berries turn black
when ripe. Small
tree or shrub.
Damp places.

4m

Red
berries

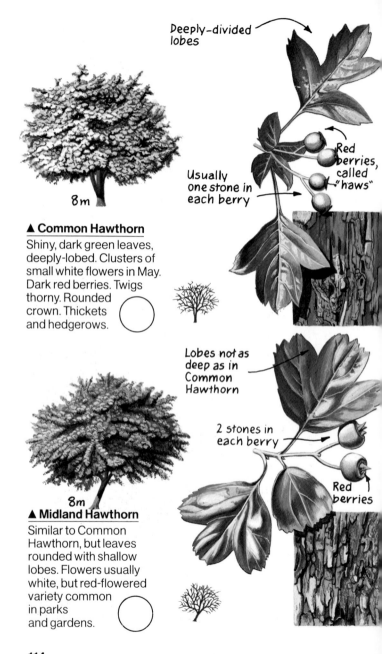

Deeply-divided lobes

Usually one stone in each berry

Red berries, called "haws"

**▲ Common Hawthorn**

Shiny, dark green leaves, deeply-lobed. Clusters of small white flowers in May. Dark red berries. Twigs thorny. Rounded crown. Thickets and hedgerows.

8 m

Lobes not as deep as in Common Hawthorn

2 stones in each berry

Red berries

**▲ Midland Hawthorn**

Similar to Common Hawthorn, but leaves rounded with shallow lobes. Flowers usually white, but red-flowered variety common in parks and gardens.

8 m

3 lobes

Red berries

## ▲ Guelder Rose

Leaves with 3-5 toothed lobes, turning russet in autumn. Clusters of white flowers, inner flowers much smaller. Red berries. Hedgerow shrub.

3m

Large outer flowers

Tiny inner flowers

## ▲ Wild Service Tree

Leaves five-lobed, turning deep red in autumn. Clusters of white flowers in May. Drab brown, speckled berries. Small rounded tree.

12m

Lowest pair of lobes are the most deeply divided

Dark grey bark becomes furrowed with age

Flower

# Identifying Winter Buds

In winter you can identify broad-leaved trees by their winter buds.

**English Oak**
Clusters of stout, light brown buds on rugged twigs.

**Turkey Oak**
Clusters of small, brown, whiskered buds.

**Red Oak**
Clusters of reddish-brown, buds on grey-green twigs with large bud at the tip.

**Ash**
Large black buds on silver-grey twigs.

**Alder**
Stalked violet buds. Male catkins often present.

**Rowan**
Large blackish end bud with tuft of white hairs.

**White Poplar**
Small, orange-brown bud covered by white felty hairs on green twigs.

**White Willow**
Slender buds enclosed in a single scale, close to pinkish downy twig.

**Common Beech**
Long pointed, copper-brown buds sticking out from brown twigs.

**Hornbeam**
Dull brown or green buds, close to fine, greyish-brown twigs.

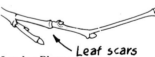

*Leaf scars*

**London Plane**
Brown, cone-shaped buds with ring scars round them.

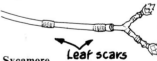

*Leaf scars*

**Sycamore**
Large green buds with dark-edged scales on stout, light brown twigs.

**English Elm**
Pointed, hairy, chocolate-brown buds on stout twigs.

**Common Walnut**
Big, black, velvety, triangle-shaped buds on stout, hollow twigs.

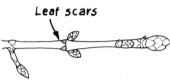

**Horse Chestnut**
Large, sticky, brown buds on stout twigs, with obvious leaf scars.

**False Acacia**
Small buds with thorns at base on grey, crooked, ribbed twigs.

**Wild Service Tree**
Flat, green buds with brown-edged scales on thick, light-brown twigs.

**Sweet Chestnut**
Rounded, reddish-brown buds on knobbly, greenish-brown twigs.

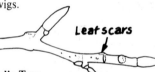

**Tulip Tree**
Flat, purplish buds with short stalk on light brown twigs.

**Wild Cherry**
Fat, shiny, red-brown buds grouped at tip of light brown twigs.

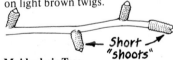

**Maidenhair Tree**
Squat, reddish-brown buds on fawn-coloured twigs.

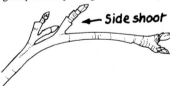

**Crab Apple**
Small, hairy, brown, triangle-shaped buds, often bent to one side, on shiny twigs.

**Common Lime**
Reddish-brown, lop-sided buds on reddish twigs.

# Bark Quiz

Name the trees these bark rubbings are from. The answers are upside-down at the bottom of the page.

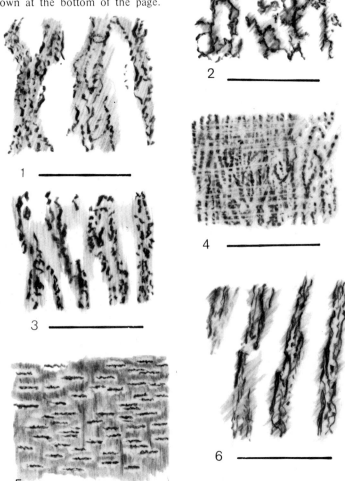

1

2

3

4

5

6

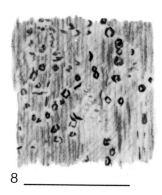

7 _____

8 _____

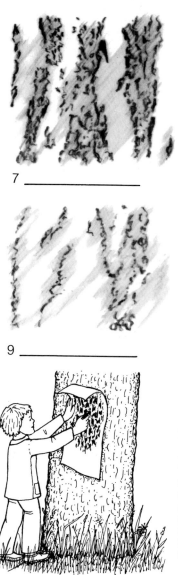

9 _____

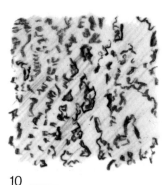

10 _____

# Making Bark Rubbings

To make bark rubbings, you need strong thin paper, wax crayons and sellotape. Tape a piece of paper against the trunk of a tree. Rub firmly up and down on the paper with the crayon until the bark pattern appears. Be careful not to tear the paper when rubbing.

# Match the Fruits to the Trees

Match the numbered fruits to the trees on which they grow. The answers are upside-down at the bottom of the opposite page.

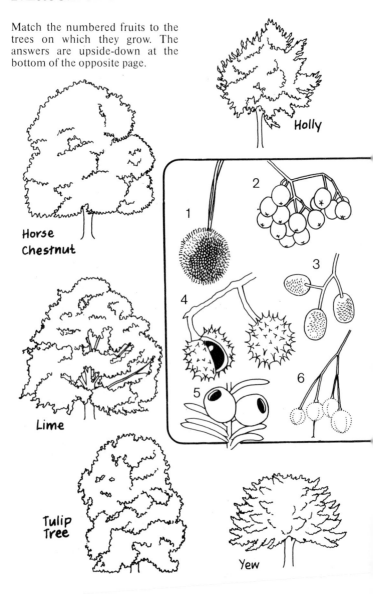

Holly

Horse Chestnut

Lime

Tulip Tree

Yew

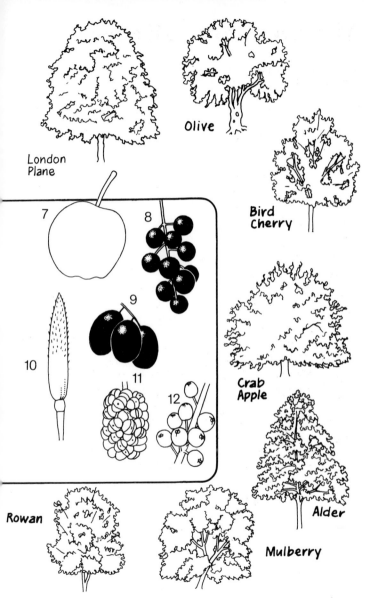

London Plane

Olive

Bird Cherry

Crab Apple

Mulberry

Alder

Rowan

7

8

9

10

11

12

1. London Plane 2. Rowan 3. Alder 4. Horse Chestnut 5. Yew 6. Lime 7. Crab Apple 8. Bird Cherry 9. Olive 10. Tulip Tree 11. Black Mulberry 12. Holly

121

# Growing Seedlings

Try growing your own tree from a seed. Pick ripe seeds from trees or from the ground. Acorns are especially easy to find and grow, but almost any fresh seed will do. Most seeds take a couple of months to sprout.

**1**

Soak the acorns or other hard nuts overnight in warm water. Take the cups off the acorns, but do not try to remove their shells.

**2**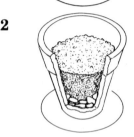

Put some stones or pebbles in the bottom of a flower pot. This will help the water to drain properly. Fill the pot with soil or compost until the pot is almost full. Place a saucer under the pot and water the soil well.

**3**

Because the seeds need plenty of room to grow, place only one seed in each pot that you have prepared. Cover the seed with a thin layer of soil. Press the soil down to make it firm. Water the soil again lightly.

**4**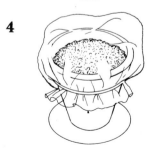

Place a plastic bag over the top of each pot and fasten it with string or a rubber band. This will help to keep the soil inside the pot moist without any watering. Place the pot on a window-sill if possible or in a sunny place. Wait for the seeds to sprout.

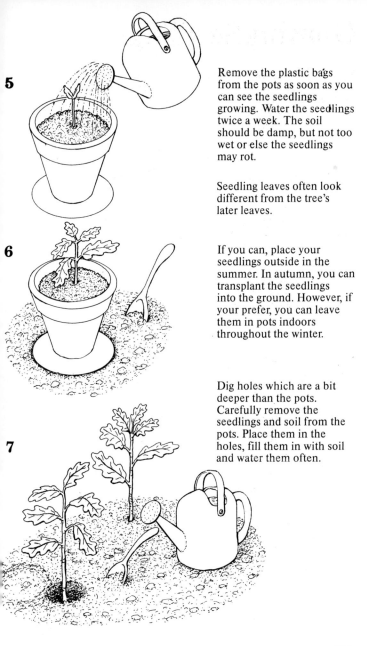

**5** Remove the plastic bags from the pots as soon as you can see the seedlings growing. Water the seedlings twice a week. The soil should be damp, but not too wet or else the seedlings may rot.

Seedling leaves often look different from the tree's later leaves.

**6** If you can, place your seedlings outside in the summer. In autumn, you can transplant the seedlings into the ground. However, if your prefer, you can leave them in pots indoors throughout the winter.

**7** Dig holes which are a bit deeper than the pots. Carefully remove the seedlings and soil from the pots. Place them in the holes, fill them in with soil and water them often.

# Books to Read

For identification: *Know Your Broadleaves* and *Know Your Conifers*. H. L. Edlin (H.M.S.O.). Two paperbacks from the Forestry Commission. Good value.
*Trees in Britain*. (Jarrold). A series of five cheap booklets, with colour photographs.
*A Field Guide to the Trees of Britain and Northern Europe*. A. Mitchell (Collins). Good, detailed reference book to carry round.
*Trees of the world*. S. Leathart (Hamlyn). Large book with colour photographs. Worth getting out of the library.
*Trees and Bushes of Europe*. O. Polunin (Oxford). Lots of colour photographs.
For reading: *The NatureTrail Book of Trees & Leaves*. I. Selberg (Usborne). Facts about trees and how they grow. Lots of projects, eg. making a tree survey and making leaf tiles. Good value.
*The World of a Tree*. A. Darlington (Faber). All about the animals and insects that live in and around trees.
*Town & Country: Growing Trees*. I. Finch (Longman). How trees grow. Cheap paperback.

# Places to Visit

These are gardens open to the public and are very good places to spot trees.
*Royal Botanic Gardens*, Kew, Richmond, Surrey.
*Regent's Park*, London.
*Hyde Park*, London.
*Royal Horticultural Society Gardens*, Wisley, Ripley, Surrey.
*Borde Hill*, Haywards Heath, Sussex.
*Royal Botanic Gardens*, Wakehurst Place, Ardingly, nr. Haywards Heath, Sussex.
*Sheffield Park*, Uckfield, Sussex.
*Winkworth Arboretum*, Godalming, Surrey.
*Syon House*, Brentford, Middx.
*Cambridge University Botanic Gardens*, Cambridge.
*Oxford University Botanic Gardens*, Oxford.
*The National Pinetum*, Bedgebury, Goudhurst, Kent.
*Savill Gardens*, Windsor, Berks.
*Bolderwood Arboretum*, New Forest, Hants.
*Exebury*, Beaulieu, Hants.
*Eastnor Castle*, Ledbury, Herefordshire.
*Stourhead*, Mere, Wilts.
*Westonbirt Arboretum*, nr. Tetbury, Glos.
*Speech House*, Coleford, Glos.
*Bath Botanic Gardens*, Bath, Avon.
*Bicton Gardens*, East Budleigh, Devon.
*Liverpool University Botanic Gardens*, Liverpool.
*Chatsworth House*, Derbyshire.
*Harlow Car Gardens*, Harrogate, Yorks.
*Bodnant Gardens*, Tal-y-cefn, Conway, Clwyd.
*Vivod Forest Garden*, Llangollen, Clwyd.
*Royal Botanic Gardens*, Edinburgh
*Inverary Castle*, Argyllshire.
*Younger Botanic Gardens*, Benmore, by Dunoon, Argyllshire
*Diana's Grove*, Blair Castle, Blair Atholl, Perthshire.

# Latin Names of Trees

Here is a list of the names of the trees in this book, in Latin. The common (English) name may vary from one part of the country to another, but the Latin name remains the same.

# Keeping a Tree Notebook

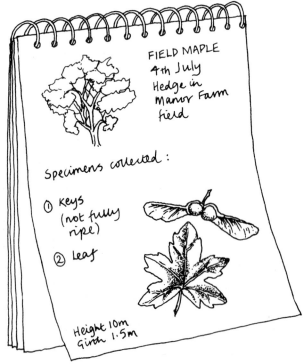

FIELD MAPLE
4th July
Hedge in
Manor Farm
field

Specimens collected:

① Keys
(not fully
ripe)

② Leaf

Height 10m
Girth 1.5m

Here is a sample page of a tree-spotter's notebook. The leaves and fruits that you collect can later be stuck into a larger scrapbook, and you can write all the details that you noticed about the tree next to them.

Make a sketch of the whole tree in your field notebook, and make a better drawing or painting later for your scrapbook. You could also take photographs and put these in the book.

Several of the books listed on page 124 tell you how to work out a tree's height. You can measure the fatness of a tree trunk (its "girth") at chest height, with a piece of string and a tape measure. This is easier if you have a friend to help you.

Make a bark rubbing, as shown on page 119, and put this in your scrapbook also. If you collect some seeds, try growing them, as explained on pages 122-3, and make notes in your book about their growth.

Even if you can only find a few different species, you can make a very interesting book about all the part of a tree, what happens to it in each season, and what makes it different from other species.

# Trees Scorecard

The trees in this scorecard are arranged in alphabetical order. When you go spotting, fill in the date at the top of one of the blank columns, and then write in that column your score, next to each tree that you see. At the end of the day, add up your scores and put the total at the bottom of the columns. Then add up your grand total.

| Name of tree | Score | Date | Date | Date | Name of tree | Score | | | |
|---|---|---|---|---|---|---|---|---|---|
| Acacia, False | 10 | | | | Cypress, Leyland | 15 | | | |
| Alder, Common | 5 | | | | Cypress, Monterey | 15 | | | |
| Alder, Grey | 15 | | | | Cypress, Nootka | 15 | | | |
| Apple, Crab | 10 | | | | Cypress, Swamp | 15 | | | |
| Ash, Common | 5 | | | | Deodar | 10 | | | |
| Ash, Manna | 15 | | | | Elm, English | 5 | | | |
| Aspen | 15 | | | | Elm, European White | 25 | | | |
| Beech, Common | 5 | | | | Elm, Wych | 5 | | | |
| Beech, Southern | 20 | | | | Fir, Douglas | 5 | | | |
| Birch, Silver | 5 | | | | Fir, European Silver | 10 | | | |
| Cedar, Atlas | 10 | | | | Fir, Grand | 15 | | | |
| Cedar, Japanese Red | 15 | | | | Fir, Greek | 20 | | | |
| Cedar of Lebanon | 10 | | | | Fir, Noble | 10 | | | |
| Cedar, Western Red | 10 | | | | Fir, Spanish | 20 | | | |
| Cherry, Bird | 10 | | | | Hemlock, Western | 10 | | | |
| Cherry, Wild | 5 | | | | Holly | 5 | | | |
| Chestnut, Horse | 5 | | | | Hornbeam | 10 | | | |
| Chestnut, Sweet | 5 | | | | Juniper | 15 | | | |
| Cypress, Italian | 20 | | | | Laburnum | 5 | | | |
| Cypress, Lawson | 5 | | | | Larch, European | 5 | | | |
| | | | | | | | | | |
| Total | | | | | Total | | | | |

| Name of tree | Score | | | | Name of tree | Score | | | |
|---|---|---|---|---|---|---|---|---|---|
| Larch, Japanese | 10 | | | | Walnut, Common | 10 | | | |
| Lime, Common | 10 | | | | Wellingtonia | 15 | | | |
| Lime, Silver | 20 | | | | Whitebeam | 10 | | | |
| Maidenhair Tree | 20 | | | | Willow, Crack | 15 | | | |
| Maple, Field | 15 | | | | Willow, Goat | 5 | | | |
| Maple, Norway | 10 | | | | Willow, White | 10 | | | |
| Mulberry, Black | 20 | | | | Yew | 5 | | | |
| Oak, Cork | 20 | | | | Pine, Stone | 25 | | | |
| Oak, English | 5 | | | | Pine, Swiss Stone | 25 | | | |
| Oak, Holm | 10 | | | | Plane, London | 10 | | | |
| Oak, Red | 10 | | | | Poplar, Black Italian | 10 | | | |
| Oak, Sessile | 5 | | | | Poplar, Grey | 10 | | | |
| Oak, Turkey | 10 | | | | Poplar, Lombardy | 10 | | | |
| Olive, Common | 25 | | | | Poplar, Western Balsam | 10 | | | |
| Palm, European Fan | 15 | | | | Poplar, White | 10 | | | |
| Pear, Common | 20 | | | | Redwood, Coast | 15 | | | |
| Pine, Aleppo | 25 | | | | Redwood, Dawn | 20 | | | |
| Pine, Chile | 10 | | | | Rowan | 5 | | | |
| Pine, Corsican | 10 | | | | Spruce, Norway | 5 | | | |
| Pine, Maritime | 15 | | | | Spruce, Sitka | 10 | | | |
| Pine, Monterey | 15 | | | | Sycamore | 5 | | | |
| Pine, Scots | 5 | | | | Tamarisk | 15 | | | |
| Pine, Shore | 10 | | | | Tulip Tree | 20 | | | |
| | Total | | | | | Total | | | |

# Part 3
# BIRDS

# Introduction to Part 3

This section of the book will help you to identify over 170 different species of birds. Some are very common indeed, and you will be able to spot them immediately. Others are more difficult to find, and you may need to gain some practice in birdwatching, and to travel to different habitats, before you can tick them off.

On pages 132 and 182-3 there are some birdwatching hints to help you begin your search. Birds are shy creatures, and you should try to follow these basic rules when watching them:

1. Approach them silently and slowly. Wear soft-soled shoes and dark, dull clothes that camouflage you.

2. Disguise your shape against a bush or tree wherever possible.

3. If there is no cover, crawl slowly towards the bird on your elbows and knees.

4. Try to approach the bird downwind (with the wind blowing towards *you*, not the bird). Then it will not hear you so easily.

5. Look for signs of birds' feathers, pellets, cracked nuts, footprints etc. when choosing a site from which to watch. Build a screen of twigs and leaves near the birds' favourite places, so that you can watch them unseen.

6. Never disturb nesting birds or their eggs. If you go too near the nest, you may cause the parents to abandon their young. Many birds are now rare because people have stolen their eggs so much. For this reason, it is now illegal to take eggs or to disturb breeding birds.

# Identifying Birds

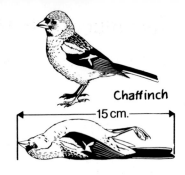

Chaffinch

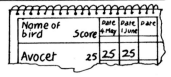

— 15 cm. —

This section is an identification guide to many of the birds you will see in Britain and Europe. The pictures show the birds perched or flying, depending on how the bird is most often spotted.

There are separate pictures of the females ( ♀ means female) if they are very different from the males ( ♂ means male). Sometimes the young, or juvenile, birds are shown too. If a bird's summer and winter plumage (feathers) are very different, both kinds of plumage are shown.

The description next to each bird tells you where to look for it and its size. A bird is measured from the tip of its beak to the tip of its tail (see diagram). Birds on the same page are not always drawn to scale.

Each time you spot a bird, make a tick in the small circle next to that bird's picture.

There is a list of special words and their meanings on page 185.

## Scorecard

There is a scorecard on pages 186-9 which gives a score for each bird you spot. A very common bird scores 5 points and a very rare one is 25 points. You can add up your scores after a day out spotting. Because some of the birds are rare in Britain, you can tick

| Name of bird | Score | Date 4 May | Date 1 June | Date |
|---|---|---|---|---|
| Avocet | 25 | 25 | 25 | |

off rare birds if you spot them on television or in a film.

## Areas Covered by this Book

The yellow area on this map shows the countries of Europe where this book can be used to spot birds. Not every bird from each country is in the book, and some birds are not found everywhere in the yellow area. The descriptions in this section always refer to Britain, unless another area is named. Britain, in this book, includes Eire. For example, the description of the Dunlin tells you that it nests on moorland in the north. This means the north of Britain. If a bird is rare in Britain, the description tells you so. Look out for it if you go abroad.

## Why Watch Birds?

Birds are everywhere, which makes watching them a good hobby. When you can name the birds you see most often, you may want to know other things about them. There is a list of books to read on page 185.

## Where to Watch Birds

Start birdwatching in your own garden, or from a window in your home. If there are only a few birds, try putting out food and water to attract more (See pages 182-3 for instructions on how to make a bird table.) When you can identify all the birds that come to your garden, look in a local park.

Watch ponds or rivers, especially early in the morning before many people are about. School playing fields, old gravel pits and even rubbish tips attract birds. If you go on holiday, you will be able to visit new habitats (places where birds live) and see new species.

## Helpful Things to Look for

Notice a bird's shape when it is flying – this will help you identify it. See if it flies in a straight line, glides, bounces or hovers. Note the colour of its plumage and any special markings. What shape is its beak? What colour are its legs and what shape are its feet?

Although bird song is important for identifying birds, it is difficult to describe, and so it is not mentioned much in this book. When you are out spotting, remember to keep your ears, as well as your eyes, open.

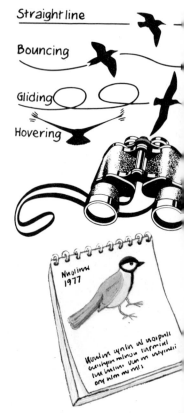

Straight line

Bouncing

Gliding

Hovering

## Binoculars

As you do more birdwatching, you will probably want to use binoculars. Visit a good shop to try out several pairs. The best sizes are 8x30 or 8x40 (never more than 10x50).

## Notebook

Keep a notebook for recording the different birds you see. Write down where and when you see them. Describe any birds you have never seen before. Make quick sketches to help you to identify them later.

**132**

# Shag, Gannet, Cormorant

### ◀ Shag ✓

Seen all year round. Nests in colonies on rocky coasts. Crest only in nesting season. Like Cormorant, dives for fish. Young are brown. 78 cm.

Shags and Cormorants fly low, close to the water

### ◀ Gannet ✓

Look out to sea close to the waves for Gannets. Plunges head first into the sea to catch fish. Young are darker. 92 cm.

### Cormorant ▼ ✓

Usually seen near the sea but sometimes inland in winter. Some have grey head and neck in the breeding season. Nests in colonies on rocky ledges. 92 cm.

← White patch in breeding season

# Geese

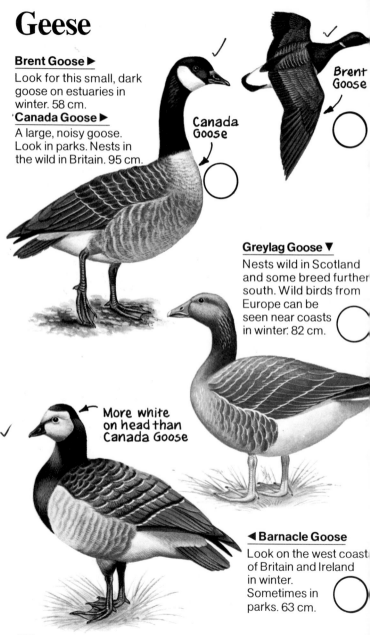

### Brent Goose ▶
Look for this small, dark goose on estuaries in winter. 58 cm.

### Canada Goose ▶
A large, noisy goose. Look in parks. Nests in the wild in Britain. 95 cm.

Brent Goose

Canada Goose

### Greylag Goose ▼
Nests wild in Scotland and some breed further south. Wild birds from Europe can be seen near coasts in winter. 82 cm.

More white on head than Canada Goose

### ◀ Barnacle Goose
Look on the west coast of Britain and Ireland in winter. Sometimes in parks. 63 cm.

# Geese, Swans

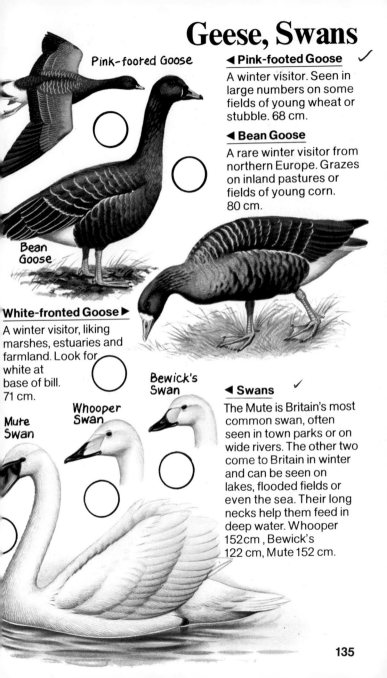

Pink-footed Goose

Bean Goose

### ◄ Pink-footed Goose ✓

A winter visitor. Seen in large numbers on some fields of young wheat or stubble. 68 cm.

### ◄ Bean Goose

A rare winter visitor from northern Europe. Grazes on inland pastures or fields of young corn. 80 cm.

### White-fronted Goose ►

A winter visitor, liking marshes, estuaries and farmland. Look for white at base of bill. 71 cm.

Bewick's Swan

Whooper Swan

Mute Swan

### ◄ Swans ✓

The Mute is Britain's most common swan, often seen in town parks or on wide rivers. The other two come to Britain in winter and can be seen on lakes, flooded fields or even the sea. Their long necks help them feed in deep water. Whooper 152 cm, Bewick's 122 cm, Mute 152 cm.

# Ducks

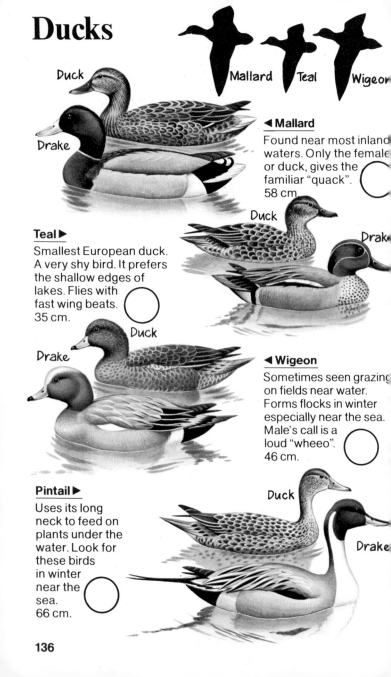

Mallard   Teal   Wigeon

Duck

Drake

### ◄ Mallard
Found near most inland waters. Only the female, or duck, gives the familiar "quack".
58 cm.

Duck

Drake

### Teal ►
Smallest European duck. A very shy bird. It prefers the shallow edges of lakes. Flies with fast wing beats.
35 cm.

Duck

Drake

### ◄ Wigeon
Sometimes seen grazing on fields near water. Forms flocks in winter especially near the sea. Male's call is a loud "wheeo".
46 cm.

### Pintail ►
Uses its long neck to feed on plants under the water. Look for these birds in winter near the sea.
66 cm.

Duck

Drake

Pintail   Shoveler   Pochard   Tufted Duck   Eider Duck

### Shoveler ▶
Likes quiet lakes and shallow water. Uses its bill to filter food. 51 cm.

Duck

Drake

Duck

Drake

### ◀ Pochard
Spends much time resting on open water and dives for food. More likely to be seen in winter. 46 cm.

### Tufted Duck ▶
Another diving duck which is more common in winter. Can sometimes be seen on town ponds. 43 cm.

Duck

Drake

Duck

Drake

### ◀ Eider
Breeds around northern sea shores. We get "eider down" from its nest. In eclipse, drakes are darker with white wing patches. 58 cm.

# Ducks

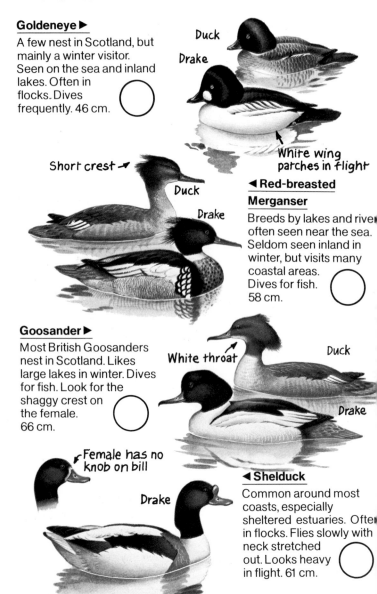

### Goldeneye ▶

A few nest in Scotland, but mainly a winter visitor. Seen on the sea and inland lakes. Often in flocks. Dives frequently. 46 cm.

Duck

Drake

White wing patches in flight

Short crest ➚

Duck

Drake

### ◀ Red-breasted
### Merganser

Breeds by lakes and river often seen near the sea. Seldom seen inland in winter, but visits many coastal areas. Dives for fish. 58 cm.

### Goosander ▶

Most British Goosanders nest in Scotland. Likes large lakes in winter. Dives for fish. Look for the shaggy crest on the female. 66 cm.

White throat

Duck

Drake

Female has no knob on bill

Drake

### ◀ Shelduck

Common around most coasts, especially sheltered estuaries. Often in flocks. Flies slowly with neck stretched out. Looks heavy in flight. 61 cm.

# Grebes, Heron, Stork

### Great Crested Grebe ▶
Found on inland waters.
Dives for fish. Seldom flies.
Beautiful courtship
displays in spring.
Sometimes seen
on sea in winter.
48 cm.

Crest expands
during display

Winter

Summer

Winter

Summer

### ◀ Little Grebe or Dabchick
Common on inland waters,
but secretive and
hard to spot. Call is
a shrill trill. 27 cm.

### Grey Heron ▶
Usually seen near water.
Nests in colonies in trees.
Eats fish, frogs, small
mammals. Stands
still for long
periods. 92 cm.

Head is drawn
back and legs
stick out
when flying

### ◀ White Stork
Very rare in Britain. Likes
wet areas. Will nest on
buildings
in Europe.
102 cm.

# Birds of Prey

### Osprey ▶

Rare summer visitor to
Britain. Some nest
in Scotland. Plunges
into water to catch fish.
Often perches on
dead trees.
56 cm.

Upper parts
dark brown

### ◀ Golden Eagle

Lives in Scottish Highlands.
Young birds have white on
wings and tail. Glides for
long distances.
Bigger than
Buzzard. 83 cm.

Long broad
wings

Wings narrower
than Buzzard's

### Red Kite ▶

This rare bird nests in oak
woods in mid-Wales.
Soars for long
periods. Rare.
62 cm.

Long forked tail

# Birds of Prey

Notice the pale wing patches

### ◀ Buzzard ✓

A large bird of prey with broad rounded wings. Often seen soaring over moors and farmland as it hunts. Rare in south and eastern England. 54 cm.

♀

Female is larger and browner than male

### parrowhawk ▶ ✓

road-winged hawk. Hunts mall birds along hedges nd woodland edges. ever hovers. emale 38 m. Male 30 cm.

♂

Long pointed wings and long tail

♀

♂

### ◀ Kestrel ✓

Well-known for the way it hovers when hunting, especially alongside motorways. Some nest in towns. Eats birds, mammals, insects. 34 cm.

# Birds of Prey

Tail shorter and wings longer than Kestrel

### ◀ Hobby
Catches flying insects and birds in the air. Summer visitor to southern England Look on heaths and downs.
33 cm.

### Peregrine ▶
Sea cliffs or inland crags. Hunts over estuaries and marshes in winter. Dives on flying birds at great speed.
38–48 cm.

### ◀ Goshawk ✓
Looks like a large Sparrowhawk. Lives in dense woods. Rare in Britain. Male 48 cm. Female 58 cm.

### Honey Buzzard ▶
Summer visitor to British woodlands. Eats mainly grubs of wasps and bees.
51–59 cm.

# Rails, Crake

### ◄ Moorhen

Water bird that lives near ponds, lakes or streams. Unafraid of people in parks, but secretive elsewhere. Juveniles are brown. 33 cm.

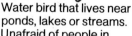

### Coot ►

Dives a lot. Prefers large lakes. Look for white bill and forehead. Young are grey with pale throats and breasts. Flocks in winter. 38 cm.

### ◄ Corncrake

Difficult to see as it lives in long grass. Repeats "crex-crex" cry monotonously, especially after dark. Rare in Britain. 27 cm.

### Water Rail ►

Secretive bird that lives in reed beds. Listen for its piglet-like squeal. Legs trail in flight. Swims for short distances. 28 cm.

# Game Birds

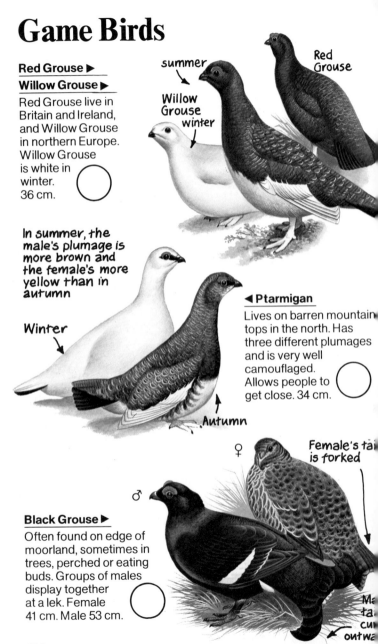

### Red Grouse ▶
### Willow Grouse ▶

Red Grouse live in
Britain and Ireland,
and Willow Grouse
in northern Europe.
Willow Grouse
is white in
winter.
36 cm.

summer

Willow
Grouse
winter

Red
Grouse

In summer, the
male's plumage is
more brown and
the female's more
yellow than in
autumn

Winter

Autumn

### ◀ Ptarmigan

Lives on barren mountain
tops in the north. Has
three different plumages
and is very well
camouflaged.
Allows people to
get close. 34 cm.

♀

Female's tail
is forked

♂

### Black Grouse ▶

Often found on edge of
moorland, sometimes in
trees, perched or eating
buds. Groups of males
display together
at a lek. Female
41 cm. Male 53 cm.

Ma
ta
cu
outwa

144

### Capercaillie ▶

This large bird lives in coniferous forests in parts of Scotland. Eats pine shoots at tips of branches.
Male 86 cm.
Female 61 cm.

♂

♀

### ◀ Partridge

Often in small groups. Likes farmland with hedges. Its call is a grating "kirr-ic".
Rarer in Ireland.
30 cm.

### Pheasant ▶

Lives on farmland with hedges. Often reared and shot as game. Roosts in trees. Nests on ground. Look for the long tail. Male 87 cm.
Female 58 cm.

♂

Cock Pheasants can vary in colour

♀

### ◀ Red-legged Partridge

Common in southern and eastern Britain. Fields and open sandy areas. Often runs rather than flies. 34 cm.

**145**

# Waders

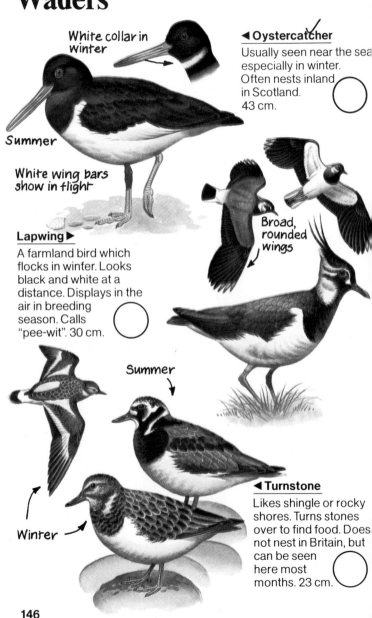

White collar in winter

Summer

White wing bars show in flight

**◄ Oystercatcher**
Usually seen near the sea especially in winter.
Often nests inland in Scotland.
43 cm.

Broad, rounded wings

**Lapwing ►**
A farmland bird which flocks in winter. Looks black and white at a distance. Displays in the air in breeding season. Calls "pee-wit". 30 cm.

Summer

Winter

**◄ Turnstone**
Likes shingle or rocky shores. Turns stones over to find food. Does not nest in Britain, but can be seen here most months. 23 cm.

When feeding, Plovers run, then pause before running on again. They bend to pick up food in one quick movement.

# Waders

## Ringed Plover ▶

Usually found near the sea, but sometimes by gravel pits inland. Likes sandy or shingle shores. Seen all the year round. 19 cm.

Summer

Juvenile

Broad white bar on wing ◢

Summer

Wing bar rarely shows in flight

## ◀ Little Ringed Plover

Summer visitor. Most common in south-east England. Likes gravel pits and shingle banks inland. Legs Legs are yellowish. 15 cm.

Northern Europe

Winter

Southern Europe

## Golden Plover ▶

Breeds on upland moors, but found in flocks on lowlands in winter. Legs are blue-grey. 28cm.

147

# Waders

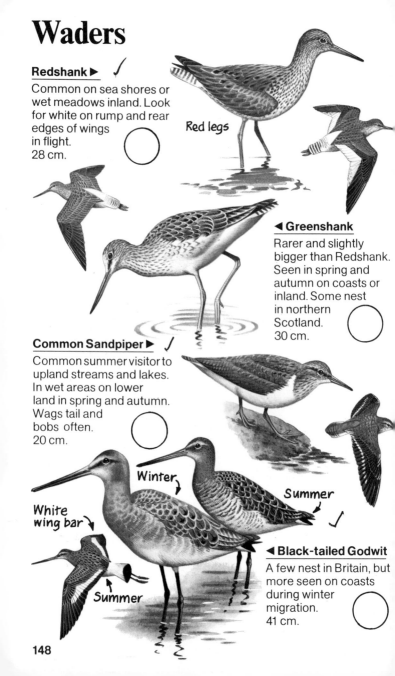

### Redshank ▶ ✓

Common on sea shores or
wet meadows inland. Look
for white on rump and rear
edges of wings
in flight.
28 cm.

Red legs

### ◀ Greenshank

Rarer and slightly
bigger than Redshank.
Seen in spring and
autumn on coasts or
inland. Some nest
in northern
Scotland.
30 cm.

### Common Sandpiper ▶ ✓

Common summer visitor to
upland streams and lakes.
In wet areas on lower
land in spring and autumn.
Wags tail and
bobs often.
20 cm.

Winter

Summer

White
wing bar

Summer

### ◀ Black-tailed Godwit

A few nest in Britain, but
more seen on coasts
during winter
migration.
41 cm.

# Waders

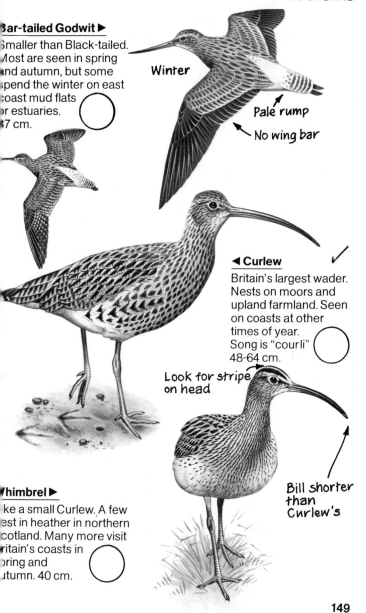

**Bar-tailed Godwit ▶**
Smaller than Black-tailed.
Most are seen in spring
and autumn, but some
spend the winter on east
coast mud flats
or estuaries.
37 cm.

Winter

Pale rump

No wing bar

**◀ Curlew**
Britain's largest wader.
Nests on moors and
upland farmland. Seen
on coasts at other
times of year.
Song is "courli"
48-64 cm.

Look for stripe
on head

Bill shorter
than
Curlew's

**Whimbrel ▶**
Like a small Curlew. A few
nest in heather in northern
Scotland. Many more visit
Britain's coasts in
spring and
autumn. 40 cm.

# Waders

Winter

Summer

### ◀ Dunlin
A common visitor to sea
shores, but nests on
moorland in the north.
Usually seen in flocks.
Beak straight
or down-
curved. 19 cm.

Winter

### Knot ▶
Seen in huge flocks in
winter. Likes sand or mud
flats in estuaries. Rare
inland. Mainly a winter
visitor. Breeds
in the Arctic.
25 cm.

### ◀ Sanderling
Runs back and forth along
water's edge on sandy
beaches where it catches
small animals.
Coasts in winter.
20 cm.

Winter

♂ Summer

♀

### Ruff ▶
Seen in spring and autumn
in Britain, but some also
winter in wet
places. Female 23
cm. Male 29 cm.

Winter
♂

# Waders

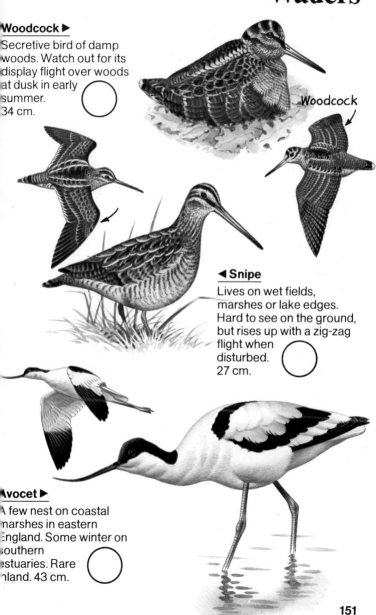

### Woodcock ▶
Secretive bird of damp woods. Watch out for its display flight over woods at dusk in early summer.
34 cm.

Woodcock

### ◀ Snipe
Lives on wet fields, marshes or lake edges. Hard to see on the ground, but rises up with a zig-zag flight when disturbed.
27 cm.

### Avocet ▶
A few nest on coastal marshes in eastern England. Some winter on southern estuaries. Rare inland. 43 cm.

# Pigeons, Doves

### Woodpigeon ▶
A common bird of farmland, woods and towns. Forms large flocks in winter. 41 cm.

White on wings

Grey rump. No white on wings

### ◀ Stock Dove
Nests in holes in trees or on rock faces. Seen feeding on the ground, often with Woodpigeons. Sometimes seen in flocks. 33 cm.

### Rock Dove ▶
Town pigeons are descended from these birds. Usually found in small groups on sea cliffs. 33 cm.

Town Pigeons

White rump

### ◀ Collared Dove
Often found in large gardens, parks or around farm buildings. Feeds mainly on grain. Sometimes seen in flocks. 30 cm.

White on tail

### Turtle Dove ▶
Summer visitor to England and Wales. Lives in open woods, parks and farmland. Listen for its purring call. 28 cm.

White margin on tail

# Auks, Fulmar

Neck and throat are white in winter

Summer

### ◀ Razorbill

Look for its flat-sided bill. Nests on cliffs and rocky shores in colonies. Winters at sea. Dives for fish. Often with Guillemots. 41 cm.

Neck and throat are white in winter ←

### Guillemot ▶

Nests on cliff ledges in large, noisy groups. Slimmer than Razorbill. Northern birds have a white eye-ring and white line on their heads. 42 cm.

Summer

### ◀ Fulmar

Nests in colonies on ledges on sea cliffs. Often glides close to waves on stiff wings. Can be seen near cliffs all round our coasts. 47 cm.

### Puffin ▶

Rocky islands and sea cliffs in the north and west. Nests between rocks or in burrows in the ground. 30 cm.

Colourful beak and reddish feet in summer

# Gulls

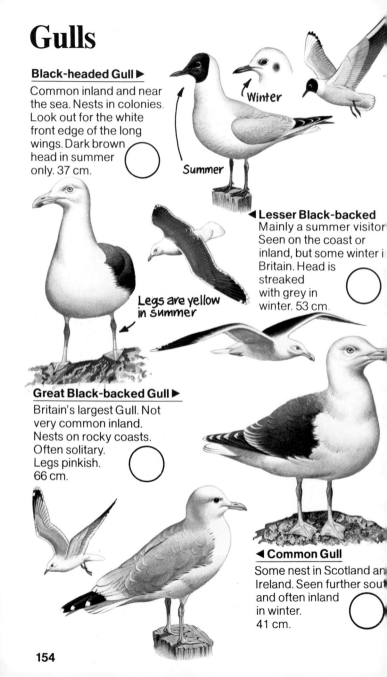

### Black-headed Gull ▶
Common inland and near the sea. Nests in colonies. Look out for the white front edge of the long wings. Dark brown head in summer only. 37 cm.

Winter

Summer

### ◀ Lesser Black-backed
Mainly a summer visitor. Seen on the coast or inland, but some winter i Britain. Head is streaked with grey in winter. 53 cm.

Legs are yellow in summer

### Great Black-backed Gull ▶
Britain's largest Gull. Not very common inland. Nests on rocky coasts. Often solitary. Legs pinkish. 66 cm.

### ◀ Common Gull
Some nest in Scotland an Ireland. Seen further sou and often inland in winter. 41 cm.

# Gull, Terns

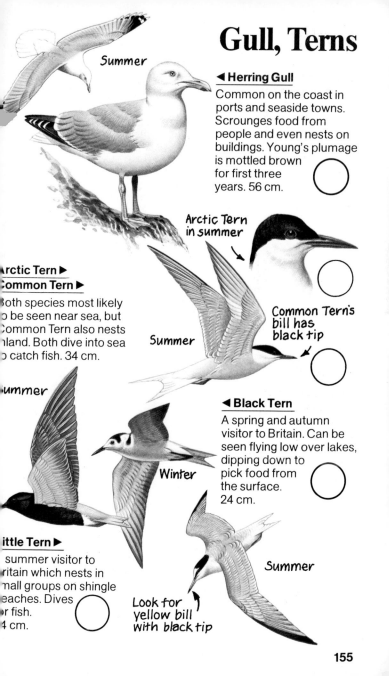

*Summer*

### ◀ Herring Gull

Common on the coast in ports and seaside towns. Scrounges food from people and even nests on buildings. Young's plumage is mottled brown for first three years. 56 cm.

*Arctic Tern in summer*

### Arctic Tern ▶
### Common Tern ▶

Both species most likely to be seen near sea, but Common Tern also nests inland. Both dive into sea to catch fish. 34 cm.

*Common Tern's bill has black tip*

*Summer*

### ◀ Black Tern

A spring and autumn visitor to Britain. Can be seen flying low over lakes, dipping down to pick food from the surface. 24 cm.

*Winter*

### Little Tern ▶

A summer visitor to Britain which nests in small groups on shingle beaches. Dives for fish. 24 cm.

*Summer*

Look for yellow bill with black tip

# Owls

### Barn Owl ▶

Its call is an eerie shriek. Often nests in old buildings or hollow trees. Hunts small mammals and roosting birds. 34 cm.

Birds with dar faces and breasts are found in nort and east Eurc

### ◀ Little Owl

Small, flat-headed ov Flies low over farmla and hunts at dusk. Ne in tree-holes. Bobs u and down when curious. 22 cm.

Bouncing flight

### Tawny Owl ▶

Calls with familiar "hoot". Hunts at night where there are woods or old trees. Eats small mammals or birds. 38 cm.

### ◀ Pygmy Owl

Smallest European owl. Found in mountain forests but not in Britain. Has a whistling "keeoo" call. Hunts small birds in flight. 16 cm.

# Owls

**Short-eared Owl ▶**

Hunts in daylight and at dusk. Likes open country where it catches voles and other small mammals. Perches on the ground. Fierce-looking. 37 cm.

**◀ Long-eared Owl**

A secretive night-hunting owl of dense conifer woods. Roosts during the day. Long "ear" tufts cannot be seen in flight. 34 cm.

**Tengmalm's Owl ▶**

Small owl that lives in forests in northern and central Europe. Very rare visitor to Britain. Hunts at night. Nests in tree-holes. cm.

**◀ Scops Owl**

Rare visitor to Britain from southern Europe. Gives its monotonous "kiu" call from a hidden perch. Hunts only at night. 19 cm.

# Hoopoe, Nightjar, Cuckoo, Kingfishe

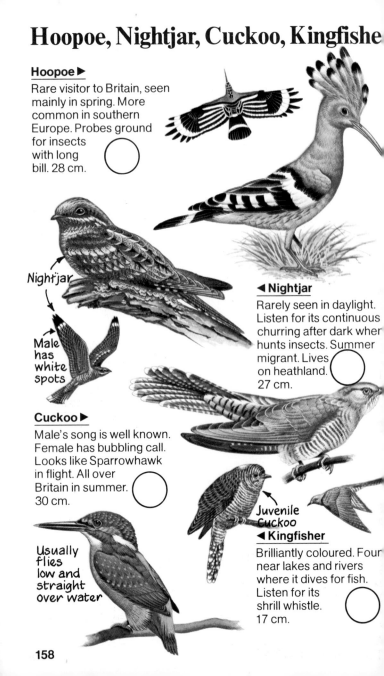

### Hoopoe ▶

Rare visitor to Britain, seen mainly in spring. More common in southern Europe. Probes ground for insects with long bill. 28 cm.

Nightjar

Male has white spots

### ◀ Nightjar

Rarely seen in daylight. Listen for its continuous churring after dark when hunts insects. Summer migrant. Lives on heathland. 27 cm.

### Cuckoo ▶

Male's song is well known. Female has bubbling call. Looks like Sparrowhawk in flight. All over Britain in summer. 30 cm.

Juvenile Cuckoo

Usually flies low and straight over water

### ◀ Kingfisher

Brilliantly coloured. Four near lakes and rivers where it dives for fish. Listen for its shrill whistle. 17 cm.

# Woodpeckers

### ▼ Great Spotted Woodpecker

Size of a Song Thrush. In woods all over Britain. Drums on trees in spring. 23 cm.

♂

Male has red crown

Female has red patch on back of head

Large white patches on wings

## ▲ Black Woodpecker

Size of a Rook. In forests in Europe, especially old pine woods. Not in Britain. Can be confused with Crow in flight. 46 cm.

### ▼ Green Woodpecker

Size of a Town Pigeon. Often feeds on ground. Open woods and parks. Quite common in England and Wales. Rare in Scotland. Laugh-like call. 32 cm.

Striped back

♂

Yellow-green rump

## ▲ Lesser Spotted Woodpecker

Sparrow-sized. Lacks white wing patches of Great Spotted. Male has red crown. Found in open woods. Not in Scotland. 14 cm.

Woodpeckers do not live in Ireland. They all have bouncing flight

# Swift, Swallow, Martins

### Swift ▶

A common migrant that visits Britain from May to August. Flies fast over towns and country in flocks. Listen for its screaming call. 17 cm.

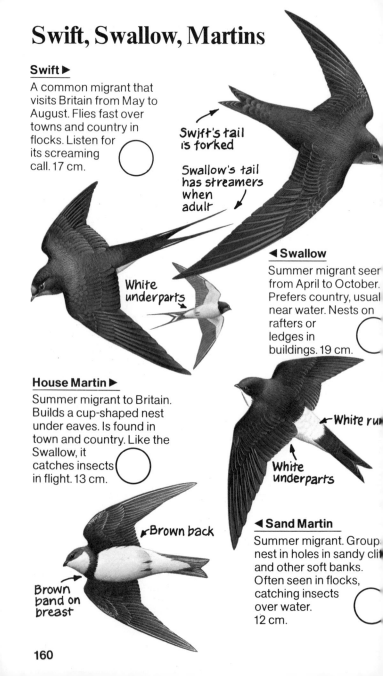

*Swift's tail is forked*

*Swallow's tail has streamers when adult*

*White underparts*

### ◀ Swallow

Summer migrant seen from April to October. Prefers country, usual near water. Nests on rafters or ledges in buildings. 19 cm.

### House Martin ▶

Summer migrant to Britain. Builds a cup-shaped nest under eaves. Is found in town and country. Like the Swallow, it catches insects in flight. 13 cm.

*White ru*

*White underparts*

*Brown back*

### ◀ Sand Martin

Summer migrant. Group nest in holes in sandy clif and other soft banks. Often seen in flocks, catching insects over water. 12 cm.

*Brown band on breast*

# Larks, Pipits, Dunnock

Pale back edges to wings

**◄ Skylark**

Lives in open country, especially farmland. It rises to a great height, hovers, and sails down, singing. 18 cm.

White outer tail feathers

**Crested Lark ►**

Seldom seen in Britain, but widespread in central and southern Europe. Likes open, often barren, areas. 17 cm.

Orange outer tail feathers

**◄ Meadow Pipit**

Most common on upland moors, but also found in fields, marshes and other open areas, especially in winter. 14.5 cm.

Sings as it "parachutes" to the ground

Song flight starts or ends on a tree or bush

**Tree Pipit ►**

Summer migrant to heaths and places with scattered trees or bushes. Often perches on branches. 15 cm.

Often flicks its wings

**◄ Dunnock**

Common, even in gardens. Feeds under bird tables. 14.5 cm.

# Wagtails

**Pied Wagtail ▶**
**White Wagtail ▶**
White Wagtail is
widespread in Europe,
but in Britain we usually
only see the Pied.
Common, even in
towns. 18 cm.

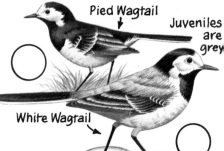

Pied Wagtail

Juveniles
are
grey

White Wagtail

All the birds on this page
wag their tails up and down.

**◀ Grey Wagtail**
Usually nests near fast-
flowing water in hilly area
Paler yellow in winter,
when it visits lowland
waters. Male has
black throat.
18 cm.

♂
Summer

Blue-headed
Wagtail
Central
Europe

♂

♂

Yellow Wagtail
Britain and Ireland

**Yellow Wagtail ▶**
**Blue-headed Wagtail ▲**
Summer visitor which likes
grassy places near water.
In Britain we usually see
only the Yellow Wagtail.
17 cm.

Ashy-headed Wagtail
Southern Europe

♂
Spanish Wagtail
Spain and Portugal

Females are
duller coloured

# Waxwing, Dipper, Wren, Shrikes

**Resembles a Starling in flight**

### ◄ Waxwing
Rare winter visitor from northern Europe. Feeds on berries and will visit gardens. 17 cm.

### Dipper ►
Likes fast-flowing rivers and streams in hilly areas. Bobs up and down on rocks in water. Submerges to find food. 18 cm.

**Northern Europe**

**Britain and Central Europe**

**Flies fast and straight on tiny, rounded wings**

### ◄ Wren
Found almost everywhere. Loud song finishes with a a trill. Never keeps still for long. 9.5 cm.

♂  ♀

### Red-backed Shrike ►
Rare summer migrant to heaths in south-east England. Catches and eats insects, small birds, etc. 17 cm.

**Stores food by sticking it on thorns**

### ◄ Great Grey Shrike
Winter visitor to open country where it feeds on birds, mammals. etc. Flies low and often hovers. 24 cm.

# Warblers

### Sedge Warbler ▶

Summer migrant. Nests in thick vegetation, usually near water, but sometimes in drier areas. Sings from cover and is often difficult to see. 13 cm.

White stripe over eye

Rump is reddish-brown

### ◀ Reed Warbler

Summer visitor. Nests in reed beds or among waterside plants, mainly in the south of England. Hard to spot. Look for it flitting over reeds. 13 cm.

### Garden Warbler ▶

Summer visitor. Sings from dense cover, and is hard to see. Likes woods with undergrowth or thick hedges. Song can be confused with Blackcap's. 14 cm.

Brown above, paler below

♂

Female's cap is reddish-brown

♀

### ◀ Blackcap

Common summer visitor to woods or places with trees. Always moving from perch to perch as it sings. 14 cm.

# Warblers

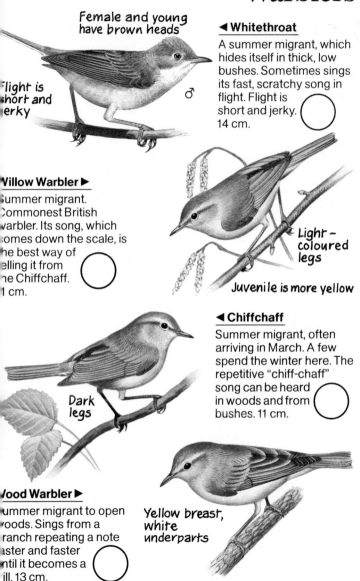

Female and young have brown heads

Flight is short and jerky

♂

### ◄ Whitethroat
A summer migrant, which hides itself in thick, low bushes. Sometimes sings its fast, scratchy song in flight. Flight is short and jerky. 14 cm.

### Willow Warbler ►
Summer migrant. Commonest British warbler. Its song, which comes down the scale, is the best way of telling it from the Chiffchaff. 11 cm.

Light-coloured legs

Juvenile is more yellow

### ◄ Chiffchaff
Summer migrant, often arriving in March. A few spend the winter here. The repetitive "chiff-chaff" song can be heard in woods and from bushes. 11 cm.

Dark legs

### Wood Warbler ►
Summer migrant to open woods. Sings from a branch repeating a note faster and faster until it becomes a trill. 13 cm.

Yellow breast, white underparts

# Flycatchers, Chats

*(handwritten notes)* overseas caught layflies air

### ◀ Pied Flycatcher
Flies after insects and catches them in the air. Also feeds on the ground. Summer migrant to some deciduous woods. 13 cm.

♂  ♀

### Whinchat ▶
Summer migrant. Found in open country. "Tic-tic" call. Perches on tops of bushes and posts. 13 cm.

♂  ♀

Flicks wings and tail

### ◀ Stonechat
Its "tak-tak" call sounds like stones being knocked together. Found on heaths with gorse, especially near the sea. 13 cm.

♀  ♂

Colour is duller in winter

### Wheatear ▶
Summer migrant to moors and barren areas, but also seen elsewhere in spring and in autumn. 15 cm.

♂  ♀

White rump and black tail

# Flycatchers, Chats

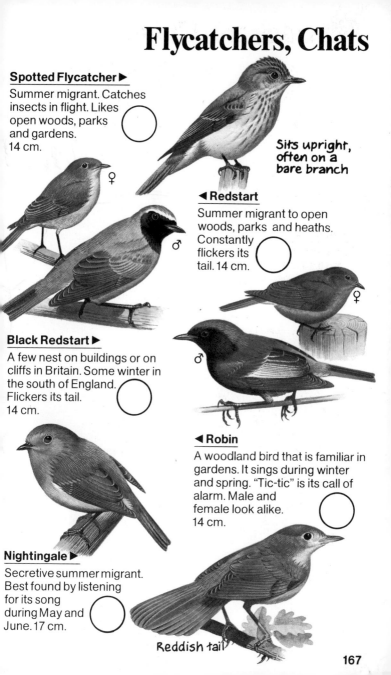

### Spotted Flycatcher ▶

Summer migrant. Catches insects in flight. Likes open woods, parks and gardens. 14 cm.

Sits upright, often on a bare branch

♀

♂

### ◀ Redstart

Summer migrant to open woods, parks and heaths. Constantly flickers its tail. 14 cm.

♀

♂

### Black Redstart ▶

A few nest on buildings or on cliffs in Britain. Some winter in the south of England. Flickers its tail. 14 cm.

### ◀ Robin

A woodland bird that is familiar in gardens. It sings during winter and spring. "Tic-tic" is its call of alarm. Male and female look alike. 14 cm.

### Nightingale ▶

Secretive summer migrant. Best found by listening for its song during May and June. 17 cm.

Reddish tail

# Thrushes, Oriole

### Fieldfare ▶

Winter visitor, but a few nest in England and Scotland. Flocks can be seen in autumn, eating berries in hedgerows.
25.5 cm.

### ◀ Ring Ouzel

Summer migrant to moors and mountains. Visits lower regions on migration. Shyer than Blackbird. Listen for loud piping call. 24 cm.

♂
♀

Young are lighter and spottier than female

♀
♂

### Blackbird ▶

Lives where there are trees and bushes, often in parks and gardens. Some Blackbirds are part albino and have some white feathers.
25 cm.

### ◀ Golden Oriole

Rare summer migrant most likely to be seen in thick woods of England or Wales. Difficult to see as it spends a lot of time in tree-tops. 24 cm.

♂
♀

# Thrushes, Starling

White stripe over eye

## ◀ Redwing

Winter migrant, but a few nest in Scotland. Seen feeding on berries in hedges or hunting worms on grass. 21 cm.

## ong Thrush ▶

ound near or in trees or
nd bushes. Well-known
r the way it breaks open
nail shells.
ften in
ardens. 23 cm.

Smaller than Mistle Thrush →

## ◀ Mistle Thrush

Large thrush found in most parts of Britain. Often seen on the ground in pastures and on moorland. 27 cm.

White under wing

White outer tail feathers

## tarling ▶

familiar garden bird. Often
osts in huge flocks.
imics songs of
her birds. 22 cm.

Juvenile

Adult in winter

# Tits

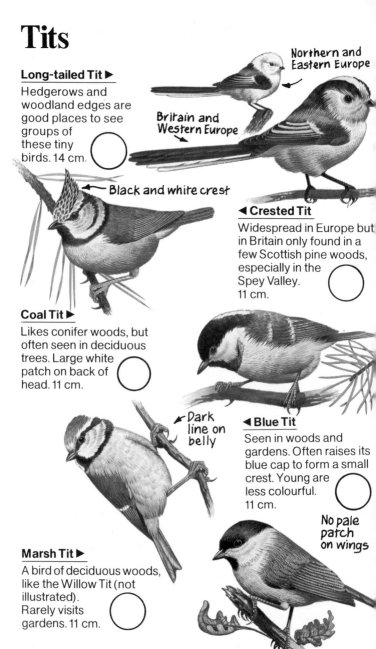

### Long-tailed Tit ▶
Hedgerows and woodland edges are good places to see groups of these tiny birds. 14 cm.

Northern and Eastern Europe

Britain and Western Europe

Black and white crest

### ◀ Crested Tit
Widespread in Europe but in Britain only found in a few Scottish pine woods, especially in the Spey Valley. 11 cm.

### Coal Tit ▶
Likes conifer woods, but often seen in deciduous trees. Large white patch on back of head. 11 cm.

Dark line on belly

### ◀ Blue Tit
Seen in woods and gardens. Often raises its blue cap to form a small crest. Young are less colourful. 11 cm.

No pale patch on wings

### Marsh Tit ▶
A bird of deciduous woods, like the Willow Tit (not illustrated). Rarely visits gardens. 11 cm.

# Tit, Nuthatch, Treecreeper, Crests

### Great Tit ▶
Largest tit. Lives in woodlands and gardens. Nests in holes in trees or will use nestboxes. 14 cm.

**Broad black band on breast**

### ◀ Nuthatch
Found in deciduous woods in England and Wales. Climbs up and down trees in a series of short hops. Very short tail. Nests in tree-holes. 14 cm.

### Treecreeper ▶
Usually seen in woods climbing up tree trunks and flying down again to search for food. Listen for its high-pitched call. 13 cm.

**White stripe over eye**

Firecrest

Goldcrest

### ◀ Firecrest
### ◀ Goldcrest
Smallest European birds. Goldcrests are often found in woods, especially of pine, all over Britain. Firecrests are much rarer. 9 cm.

# Finches

### Chaffinch ▶
Likely to be found wherever there are trees and bushes, including gardens. Often flocks with other finches in winter.
15 cm.

♀

♂

♀

### ◀ Brambling
Winter migrant from northern Europe. Flocks feed on grain and seeds. Likes fruit from beech trees.
15 cm.

Male's head is brown in winter ↘

♂

### Greenfinch ▶
A frequent visitor to gardens, especially in winter. Likely to nest wherever there are trees and bushes. 15 cm.

♀

♂

### ◀ Siskin
A small finch. Nests in conifers. Visits gardens in winter to feed on peanuts.
11 cm.

♀

♂

# Finches

### ◄ Bullfinch
Often found on edges of woods, and in hedges or gardens. Eats seeds, but is a pest in orchards where it strips buds from fruit trees. 15 cm.

♀

← White rump shows in flight

♂

♀

### Linnet ►
Lives on heathland and farmland, but also found in towns, where it may visit gardens. Feeds on the seeds of weeds. Flocks in winter. 13 cm.

Mealy Redpoll

↓

Lesser Redpoll

### ◄ Lesser Redpoll
### ◄ Mealy Redpoll
The Lesser Redpoll is common in birch woods and forestry plantations in Britain. The Mealy lives in northern Europe. 12 cm.

### Goldfinch ►
Feeds on thistle seeds and other weed seeds in open spaces. Nests in trees. cm.

Yellow wing bar

173

# Crossbill, Crows

♀ ♂

Sparrow-sized

### ◄ Crossbill

Nests in Scottish pine wood
Rare elsewhere. Eats
seeds from pine
cones. 16 cm.

### Jay ►

Secretive woodland
bird. Will visit gardens.
Listen for its harsh
screeching call. Look
for white rump
in flight.
32 cm.

### Raven ►

This large crow lives in
wild rocky areas or on
rocky coasts. Look for its
wedge-shaped tail
and huge bill.
Croaks. 64 cm.

Grey on
head

### Jackdaw ►

Small member of the crow
family. Found where there
are old trees, old buildings
or cliffs. Nests in colonies.
Often seen
with Rooks.
33 cm.

# Crows

### ◄ Carrion Crow
### ◄ Hooded Crow

Carrion is seen alone or in pairs. Hooded Crows form flocks. Carrion is more widespread than Hooded 47 cm.

Carrion Crow — England, Wales and southern Scotland

Hooded Crow — Northern Scotland and Ireland

### Rook ►

Nests in "rookeries" in tops of trees. Is usually seen in flocks and likes farmland. Young lack bare skin round beak. Voice is a harsh "kaw". 46 cm.

Baggy thigh feathers

### ◄ Magpie

Seen in both town and country. Eats many eggs and young birds in spring. Forms flocks in winter. 46 cm.

# Sparrows, Buntings

### House Sparrow ▶

Very familiar bird. Lives near houses and even in city centres, where it eats scraps, etc. Often seen in flocks.
15 cm.

Brown cap and smudge below eye →

Male and female look alike

### ◀ Tree Sparrow

Usually nests in holes in trees or cliffs. Less common than House Sparrows in towns, but sometimes flocks with them in winter. 14 cm.

♀

### Yellowhammer ▶

Common in open country, especially farmland. Feeds on the ground. Forms flocks in winter. Sings from the tops of bushes.
17 cm.

♂

♀

♀

### ◀ Reed Bunting

Most common near water, but some nest in dry areas with long grass. Sometimes visits bird-tables in winter.
15 cm.

♂

### Corn Bunting ▶

Quite common in cornfields. Sings from posts, bushes or overhead wires.
18 cm.

# Colour the Birds

Can you identify these birds and colour them correctly? Their names are upside-down at the bottom of the page.

1 _____

2 _____

3 _____

4 _____

1. Pheasant (male) 2. Kingfish
3. Blue Tit 4. Collared Dove

# Find the Feet

Can you match the pictures of feet with the correct birds? The answers are upside-down at the bottom of the opposite page.

**Lesser Spotted Woodpecker** ___

**Cormorant**

___

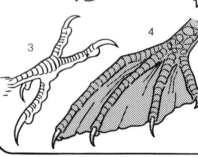

**Kingfisher** ___

**Mallard** ___

178

Robin

Golden Eagle

5

6

7

8

9

Tawny Owl

Coot

Oystercatcher

1. Coot 2. Oystercatcher 3. Lesser Spotted Woodpecker 4. Cormorant 5. Tawny Owl 6. Kingfisher 7. Golden Eagle 8. Mallard 9. Robin

**179**

# Name the Birds

Look carefully at the shapes of these birds and try to identify them. Their names are upside-down at the bottom of the opposite page.

1 ——————————

2 ——————————

3 ——————————

4 ——————————

5

6

7

8

9

1. Swift 2. Woodcock 3. Avocet 4. Capercaillie 5. Swallow 6. Gannet 7. Black Grouse (male) 8. Lapwing 9. Great Crested Grebe

# Making a Bird Table

Why not make a bird table for your garden or to attach to a window-sill? This is a good way to attract birds and you will be helping them to survive the winter.

Suitable foods are peanuts (not salted), pieces of apple, cereals, bacon rinds, biscuit crumbs, raisins, sunflower seeds, cooked potato and hardened fat.

Feed garden birds between October and March. There should be enough natural food for them in the summer, and some of the foods mentioned above can be harmful to young birds born in the spring.

If you put food out every day, do not stop suddenly, especially if the weather is cold, because the birds will be relying on your food supply.

Clean the bird table regularly with hot water and remove bits of old food.

These diagrams show you how to make a simple bird table. You will need: A piece of thick plywood (40 cm square), four lengths of softwood (2 cm x 2 cm x 30 cm long), eight screws and a screwdriver, glue, wood preservative and a paint-brush, nylon string and four screw eyes. You can buy these at a hardware shop.

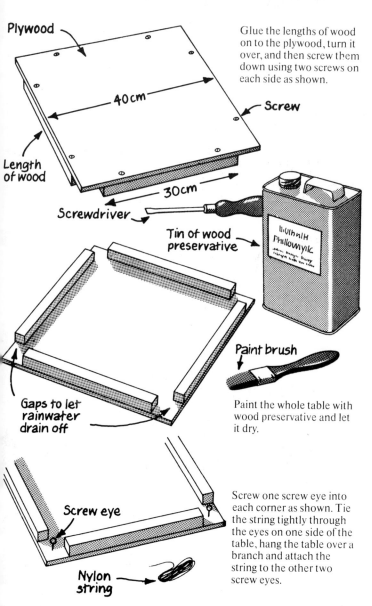

**Plywood**

**Screw**

Glue the lengths of wood on to the plywood, turn it over, and then screw them down using two screws on each side as shown.

40cm

**Length of wood**

30cm

**Screwdriver**

**Tin of wood preservative**

**Paint brush**

**Gaps to let rainwater drain off**

Paint the whole table with wood preservative and let it dry.

**Screw eye**

**Nylon string**

Screw one screw eye into each corner as shown. Tie the string tightly through the eyes on one side of the table, hang the table over a branch and attach the string to the other two screw eyes.

# Garden Bird Survey

Make a survey of the birds that visit your table, or wherever you put food out for them. You will soon learn when to expect certain birds. Try to find out which birds feed on natural foods, such as worms and berries, and which eat the scraps you put out for them. You may also be able to watch birds collecting material to build their nests. The best time to see birds is in the early morning.

The chart on this page is an example of a garden bird survey. Make a survey of the birds that visit your garden in an exercise book or in a loose leaf binder. You can make a weekly bird check instead of a monthly one if you prefer. Keep your survey up-to-date for two years to compare appearances and lengths of stay of migrating birds

| NAMES OF BIRDS SEEN | TICK OFF MONTHS YOU SEE BIRDS J F M A M J J A S O N D | FOODS EATEN | | DO THEY DRINK? | DO THEY BATHE? | WHERE THEY NEST |
|---|---|---|---|---|---|---|
| | | FOOD YOU PUT OUT | NATURAL FOOD | | | |
| HOUSE SPARROW | ✓ ✓ ✓ ✓ | BREAD | | ✓ | ✓ | UNDER EAVES |
| ROBIN | | | | | | |
| BLUE TIT | | | | | | |
| GREAT TIT | | | | | | |
| STARLING | | | | | | |
| DUNNOCK | | | | | | |
| BLACKBIRD | | | | | | |
| SONG THRUSH | | | | | | |
| GREENFINCH | | | | | | |
| COLLARED DOVE | | | | | | |
| PIED/WHITE WAGTAIL | | | | | | |
| HOUSE MARTIN | | | | | | |
| SWALLOW | | | | | | |
| CHAFFINCH | | | | | | |

# Glossary

**Breeding season** − the time of year when a pair of birds build a nest, mate, lay eggs and look after their young.

**Colony** - a group of birds of the same species nesting close together.

**Conifers** − trees, such as pines and firs, that bear cones, have needle-like leaves and are usually evergreen.

**Courtship display** − when a male bird attracts a mate. Some birds show off their plumage; others put on a "display" in the air.

**Cover** - hedges, bushes, thick grass − anywhere that birds hide themselves.

**Crown** − the top of a bird's head.

**Juvenile** − a young bird which has left the nest and whose plumage is not yet the same as its parents'.

**Lek** − an area where male birds gather to display to females in the breeding season.

**Migration** − the regular movement of birds from one place to another, from the breeding area to the area where they spend the winter. Migrating birds are called migrants or visitors.

**Moult** − when birds shed their old feathers and grow new ones. All birds do this at least once a year. In ducks, the duller plumage that remains after moulting is called **eclipse** plumage.

**Roost** − sleep. A roost is a place where birds sleep.

**Rump** − the lower back and base of the tail of a bird.

**Species** - a group of birds that all look alike and behave in the same way, e.g. the Herring Gull is the name of one species, group.

# Books to Read

*The Pocket Oxford Book of Birds.* Bruce Campbell (OUP)
*The RSPB Guide to British Birds.* D. Saunders (Hamlyn). Two useful field guides to British birds.
*A Field Guide to the Birds of Britain and Europe.* R. T. Peterson, G. Mountford and P. A. D. Hollom (Collins). A very reliable field guide.
*The Naturetrail Book of Birdwatching.* Malcolm Hart (Usborne). Useful birdwatching tips and ideas for studying birds.
*Birds.* Christopher Perrins. (Collins Countryside Series). How birds live and the problems they face.
*Book of British Birds.* (AA/Reader's Digest). Lots of information and pictures.
*The New Birdtable Book.* Tony Soper (hardback David & Charles/paperback Pan). How to find out more about garden birds.
*Bird Count.* Humphrey Dobinson (hardback Kestrel/paperback Peacock). Practical ways to study birds.
You can buy records and tapes of bird song, or you may be able to borrow them from your library. If you want a catalogue of available records, write to the R.S.P.B., The Lodge, Sandy, Bedfordshire.

# Birds Scorecard

The birds in this scorecard are arranged in alphabetical order. When you go spotting, fill in the date at the top of one of the blank columns, and then write in that column your score, next to each bird that you see. At the end of the day, add up your scores and put the total at the bottom of the columns. Then add up your grand total.

| Name of bird | Score | Date | Date | Date | Name of bird | Score | | | |
|---|---|---|---|---|---|---|---|---|---|
| Avocet | 25 | | | | Dove, Collared | 10 | | | |
| Blackbird | 5 | | | | Dove, Rock | 25 | | | |
| Blackcap | 15 | | | | Dove, Stock | 15 | | | |
| Brambling | 15 | | | | Dove, Turtle | 15 | | | |
| Bullfinch | 10 | | | | Duck, Tufted | 10 | | | |
| Bunting, Corn | 15 | | | | Dunlin | 10 | | | |
| Bunting, Reed | 15 | | | | Dunnock | 5 | | | |
| Buzzard | 15 | | | | Eagle, Golden | 20 | | | |
| Buzzard, Honey | 25 | | | | Eider | 15 | | | |
| Capercaillie | 20 | | | | Fieldfare | 10 | | | |
| Chaffinch | 5 | | | | Firecrest | 20 | | | |
| Chiffchaff | 10 | | | | Flycatcher, Pied | 15 | | | |
| Coot | 10 | | | | Flycatcher, Spotted | 10 | | | |
| Cormorant | 15 | | | | Fulmar | 15 | | | |
| Corncrake | 20 | | | | Gannet | 20 | | | |
| Crossbill | 15 | | | | Godwit, Bar-tailed | 20 | | | |
| Crow, Carrion | 10 | | | | Godwit, Black-tailed | 20 | | | |
| Crow, Hooded | 15 | | | | Goldcrest | 10 | | | |
| Cuckoo | 10 | | | | Goldeneye | 15 | | | |
| Curlew | 15 | | | | Goldfinch | 10 | | | |
| Dipper | 15 | | | | Goosander | 20 | | | |
| Total | | | | | Total | | | | |

| Name of bird | Score | | | | Name of bird | Score | | | |
|---|---|---|---|---|---|---|---|---|---|
| Goose, Barnacle | 20 | | | | Jackdaw | 10 | | | |
| Goose, Bean | 25 | | | | Jay | 10 | | | |
| Goose, Brent | 20 | | | | Kestrel | 10 | | | |
| Goose, Canada | 10 | | | | Kingfisher | 15 | | | |
| Goose, Greylag | 15 | | | | Kite, Red | 25 | | | |
| Goose, Pink-footed | 20 | | | | Knot | 15 | | | |
| Goose, White-fronted | 20 | | | | Lapwing | 10 | | | |
| Goshawk | 25 | | | | Lark, Crested | 25 | | | |
| Grebe, Great-Crested | 15 | | | | Linnet | 10 | | | |
| Grebe, Little | 15 | | | | Magpie | 10 | | | |
| Greenfinch | 10 | | | | Mallard | 5 | | | |
| Greenshank | 20 | | | | Martin, House | 10 | | | |
| Grouse, Black | 15 | | | | Martin, Sand | 15 | | | |
| Grouse, Red | 15 | | | | Merganser, Red-breasted | 20 | | | |
| Grouse, Willow | 25 | | | | Moorhen | 5 | | | |
| Guillemot | 15 | | | | Nightingale | 15 | | | |
| Gull, Black-headed | 5 | | | | Nightjar | 15 | | | |
| Gull, Common | 15 | | | | Nuthatch | 15 | | | |
| Gull, Great Black-backed | 15 | | | | Oriole, Golden | 20 | | | |
| Gull, Herring | 5 | | | | Osprey | 25 | | | |
| Gull, Lesser Black-backed | 10 | | | | Ouzel, Ring | 15 | | | |
| Heron, Grey | 10 | | | | Owl, Barn | 15 | | | |
| Hobby | 20 | | | | Owl, Little | 15 | | | |
| Hoopoe | 25 | | | | Owl, Long-eared | 20 | | | |
| Total | | | | | Total | | | | |

| Name of bird | Score | | | | Name of bird | Score | | | |
|---|---|---|---|---|---|---|---|---|---|
| Owl, Pygmy | 25 | | | | Redpoll, Mealy | 25 | | | |
| Owl, Scops | 25 | | | | Redshank | 10 | | | |
| Owl, Short-eared | 20 | | | | Redstart | 15 | | | |
| Owl, Tawny | 15 | | | | Redstart, Black | 20 | | | |
| Owl, Tengmalm's | 25 | | | | Redwing | 10 | | | |
| Oystercatcher | 15 | | | | Robin | 5 | | | |
| Partridge | 10 | | | | Rook | 10 | | | |
| Partridge, Red-legged | 15 | | | | Ruff | 20 | | | |
| Peregrine | 20 | | | | Sanderling | 15 | | | |
| Pheasant | 5 | | | | Sandpiper, Common | 15 | | | |
| Pigeon, Town | 5 | | | | Shag | 15 | | | |
| Pintail | 20 | | | | Shelduck | 15 | | | |
| Pipit, Meadow | 10 | | | | Shoveler | 15 | | | |
| Pipit, Tree | 15 | | | | Shrike, Great Grey | 25 | | | |
| Plover, Golden | 15 | | | | Shrike, Red-backed | 25 | | | |
| Plover, Little Ringed | 20 | | | | Siskin | 15 | | | |
| Plover, Ringed | 15 | | | | Skylark | 10 | | | |
| Pochard | 15 | | | | Snipe | 15 | | | |
| Ptarmigan | 20 | | | | Sparrow, House | 5 | | | |
| Puffin | 20 | | | | Sparrow, Tree | 15 | | | |
| Rail, Water | 15 | | | | Sparrowhawk | 15 | | | |
| Raven | 15 | | | | Starling | 5 | | | |
| Razorbill | 15 | | | | Stonechat | 15 | | | |
| Redpoll, Lesser | 15 | | | | Stork, White | 25 | | | |
| Total | | | | | Total | | | | |

| Name of bird | Score | | | | Name of bird | Score | | | |
|---|---|---|---|---|---|---|---|---|---|
| Swallow | 10 | | | | Wagtail, Pied | 10 | | | |
| Swan, Bewick's | 20 | | | | Wagtail, White | 25 | | | |
| Swan, Mute | 10 | | | | Wagtail, Yellow | 15 | | | |
| Swan, Whooper | 20 | | | | Warbler, Garden | 15 | | | |
| Swift | 10 | | | | Warbler, Reed | 15 | | | |
| Teal | 15 | | | | Warbler, Sedge | 15 | | | |
| Tern, Arctic | 15 | | | | Warbler, Willow | 10 | | | |
| Tern, Black | 20 | | | | Warbler, Wood | 15 | | | |
| Tern, Common | 15 | | | | Waxing | 20 | | | |
| Tern, Little | 20 | | | | Wheatear | 15 | | | |
| Thrush, Mistle | 10 | | | | Whimbrel | 20 | | | |
| Thrush, Song | 5 | | | | Whinchat | 15 | | | |
| Tit, Blue | 5 | | | | Whitethroat | 15 | | | |
| Tit, Coal | 10 | | | | Wigeon | 15 | | | |
| Tit, Crested | 20 | | | | Woodcock | 15 | | | |
| Tit, Great | 5 | | | | Woodpecker, Black | 25 | | | |
| Tit, Long-tailed | 10 | | | | Woodpecker, Great Spotted | 10 | | | |
| Tit, Marsh | 15 | | | | Woodpecker, Green | 15 | | | |
| Treecreeper | 10 | | | | Woodpecker, Lesser Spotted | 20 | | | |
| Turnstone | 15 | | | | Woodpigeon | 5 | | | |
| Wagtail, Blue-headed | 25 | | | | Wren | 5 | | | |
| Wagtail, Grey | 15 | | | | Yellowhammer | 10 | | | |
| Total | | | | | Total | | | | |

Grand Total

# Index

## Part 1 – Flowers

# Part 3 – Birds

# Part 2 – Trees